Sharpen Up!

New York Mathematics

BOOK 8

Buckle Down
PUBLISHING COMPANY

ACKNOWLEDGMENT

Intermediate Learning Standards from the University of the State of New York, the State Education Department. Used with permission.

ISBN 0-7836-1806-9

Catalog #SU NY8M 1   2 3 4 5 6 7 8 9 10

President and Publisher: Douglas J. Paul, Ph.D.; Editorial Director: John Hansen; Senior Editor: Carmen P. Sosa, Ph.D.; Editor: Antionette S. McCarthy; Production Director: Jennifer Booth; Art Director: Chris Wolf; Graphic Design: Cindy Place.

TABLE OF CONTENTS

unit 1

Number and Numeration

Lesson 1: Number Sense

Lesson 2: Number Theory

Lesson 3: Ordering Numbers

Lesson 1: Number Sense

In this lesson, you will learn to represent and use numbers in a variety of equivalent forms.

Numbers with Exponents

An **exponent** tells how many times to multiply a base number by itself. Exponential notation is a short way of writing repeated factors.

$$\text{base (factor)} \rightarrow 2^3 = 2 \times 2 \times 2 = 8 \leftarrow \text{exponent}$$

When working with exponents, remember the following rules:

1. Any base number (except zero) with zero as the exponent equals 1.

$$10^0 = 1 \qquad 5^0 = 1 \qquad 25{,}000{,}000^0 = 1$$

2. A base number with 1 as the exponent equals the same number.

$$10^1 = 10 \qquad 5^1 = 5 \qquad 25{,}000{,}000^1 = 25{,}000{,}000$$

3. A negative number squared equals a positive number.

$$(^-3)^2 = {}^-3 \times {}^-3 = 9$$

PRACTICE

Directions: Complete the following.

1. $4^2 =$ _____

2. $5 \times 5 \times 5 =$ _____ in exponential notation

3. $81 =$ _____ in exponential notation

4. $3^3 =$ _____

Numbers in Scientific Notation

Scientific notation is a system of writing numbers. It is often used to write very large or very small numbers. A number in scientific notation is written as a number between 1 and 10 multiplied by powers of 10.

Powers of Ten	
Positive	**Negative**
$10^1 = 10$	$10^{-1} = 0.1$
$10^2 = 100$	$10^{-2} = 0.01$
$10^3 = 1,000$	$10^{-3} = 0.001$
$10^4 = 10,000$	$10^{-4} = 0.0001$
$10^5 = 100,000$	$10^{-5} = 0.00001$
and so on . . .	and so on . . .

Changing numbers from standard form to scientific notation

 **Example**

► Write 3,945,600 in scientific notation.

Step 1: Move the decimal point to the *left* until you have a number between 1 and 10.

3 945600.

3.945600

Step 2: Count the number of places you moved the decimal point to the *left*.

In this example, the decimal point was moved 6 places to the left.

Step 3: Use that number as an exponent to show the power of 10.

10^6

Step 4: Write an expression with the decimal number (from Step 1) multiplied by the power of ten (from Step 3).

3.9456×10^6

Changing from scientific notation to standard form

To change a number written in scientific notation with a positive power of 10 to standard form, move the decimal point to the *right*. The exponent tells you the number of places to move the decimal point.

 **Example**

 $6.173 \times 10^7 = 61{,}730{,}000$

Writing decimals in scientific notation

 **Example**

> Write .000045100 in scientific notation.

Step 1: Move the decimal point to the *right* until you have a number between 1 and 10.

0.000045100

4.51

Step 2: Count the number of places you moved the decimal point to the *right*.

In this example, the decimal point was moved 5 places to the right.

Step 3: Use that number as a *negative* exponent to show the power of ten.

10^{-5}

Step 4: Write an expression with the decimal number (from Step 1) multiplied by the power of ten (from Step 3).

4.51×10^{-5}

To change a number written in scientific notation with a negative power of 10 to standard form, move the decimal point to the *left*. The exponent tells you the number of places to move the decimal point.

$9.232 \times 10^{-4} = 0.0009232$

☰ PRACTICE

Directions: Write the following numbers in scientific notation.

1. 0.29025   _____

2. 5033   _____

Directions: Change the scientific notation to standard form.

3. 2.81168×10^{-3} _____

4. 8.7×10^{8} _____

Numbers as Fractions, Decimals, and Percents

Fractions, decimals, and percents can be thought of as different, but related, ways of saying things mathematically. Their relationships make it possible for us to:

- write a **fraction** as a percent or a decimal,
- write a **percent** as a fraction or a decimal, and
- write a **decimal** as a fraction or a percent.

Percent comes from a Latin phrase meaning "per hundred." So, when you see 54%, you can think of it as "54 per hundred." This also can be expressed as the fraction $\frac{54}{100}$ and as the decimal 0.54. No matter which way you write it: 54%, $\frac{54}{100}$, or 0.54, it means the same thing—54 parts of a whole. These are **equivalent** expressions.

Writing Decimals for Percents

To change a **decimal to a percent**, move the decimal point to the *left* two places and drop the percent symbol.

☰ Example

▶ Write a decimal for 63%.

63% = 0.63

If the percent is smaller than 10, you'll need to insert a zero in the decimal number to hold the tenths place.

 Example

▶ Write a decimal for 9%.

9% = 0.09

Another way to change a percent to a fraction or decimal is to divide by 100.

 Example

▶ Write a decimal for 74%.

$74\% = \frac{74}{100} = 0.74$

To change a **percent to a decimal**, do the opposite: Move the decimal point two places to the *right* and add the percent symbol.

 Examples

▶ A. Write a percent for 0.42.

0.42 = 42%

B. Write a percent for 0.008.

0.008 = 0.8%

You can also multiply by 100 to change a percent to a decimal.

 Example

▶ Write a percent for 0.37.

$0.37 \times 100 = 37\%$

 PRACTICE

Directions: Write a decimal for each percent.

1. 37.9% = _____

2. 4.4% = _____

3. 213% = _____

Directions: Write a percent for each decimal.

4. 0.234 = _____

5. 0.92 = _____

6. 0.001 = _____

Writing Fractions for Percents

Remember that percent is another way of saying "per hundred." When you want to change a percent to a fraction, put it in the form of a fraction that has 100 as the denominator. Then reduce it to lowest terms.

 Examples

   ▶ A. Write a fraction for 71%.

$$71\% = \frac{71}{100}$$

B. Write a fraction for 38%.

$$38\% = \frac{38}{100} = \frac{19}{50} \text{ (lowest terms)}$$

C. Write a fraction for $37\frac{1}{2}\%$.

$$37\frac{1}{2} \div 100$$

$$37\frac{1}{2} \times \frac{1}{100}$$

$$\frac{75}{2} \times \frac{1}{100} = \frac{75}{200} = \frac{3}{8}$$

≡ PRACTICE

Directions: Write a fraction in lowest terms for each percent.

1. 46% = _____

2. 12% = _____

3. 88% = _____

Writing Decimals and Percents for Fractions and Mixed Numbers

When you want to change a fraction to a decimal, divide the numerator by the denominator.

 **Example**

> Write a decimal for $\frac{1}{6}$.

$$
\begin{array}{r}
0.166 \\
6 \overline{)1.000} \\
-6\!\downarrow\!\downarrow \\
\hline
40\!\downarrow \\
-36\!\downarrow \\
\hline
40 \\
-36 \\
\hline
4
\end{array}
$$

$\frac{1}{6} = 0.17$ (Rounded to the nearest hundredth.)

To change a fraction or mixed number to a percent, first divide the fraction to get a decimal, then multiply the decimal by 100.

Example

> Write a percent for $5\frac{1}{4}$.

$$5\frac{1}{4} = \frac{21}{4}$$

$$
\begin{array}{r}
5.25 \\
4 \overline{)21.00} \\
-20\!\downarrow\!\downarrow \\
\hline
1\,0\!\downarrow \\
-8\!\downarrow \\
\hline
20 \\
-20 \\
\hline
0
\end{array}
$$

$$5\frac{1}{4} = 5.25$$

$$5.25 \times 100 = 525\%$$

Some fractions, when converted to decimals, go on for several decimal places. To convert such a fraction to a percent, carry the division of the fraction to four decimal places. Next, round to the nearest thousandth, and finally, write the quotient in percent form.

Example

▶ Write a percent for $\frac{3}{11}$.

$$
\begin{array}{r}
0.2727 \\
11\overline{\smash)3.0000} \\
-2\,2\downarrow\downarrow\downarrow \\
\hline
80\downarrow\downarrow \\
-\ 77\downarrow\downarrow \\
\hline
30\downarrow \\
-\ 22\downarrow \\
\hline
80 \\
-\ 77 \\
\hline
3
\end{array}
$$

$0.2727 = 27.3\%$ (Rounded to the nearest tenth.)

$\frac{3}{11} = 27.3\%$

 Remember that 100% equals 1. If the fraction you begin working with is less than 1, your final percent must be less than 100. If it isn't, go back and check your work.

PRACTICE

Directions: Write a percent for each fraction or mixed number. Round your answer to the nearest tenth.

1. $\frac{1}{7} =$ _____

2. $\frac{6}{13} =$ _____

3. $3\frac{3}{4} =$ _____

Lesson 2: Number Theory

This lesson reviews factors and multiples. **Factors** are numbers that are multiplied. Answers to multiplication problems are called **products**.

Common Multiples

Multiples of a number are the products that result from multiplying that number by any whole number.

 Example

Multiply 5 by the whole numbers 0, 1, 2, 3, 4, 5, . . .

$5 \times 0 = 0$　　$5 \times 1 = 5$　　$5 \times 2 = 10$
$5 \times 3 = 15$　$5 \times 4 = 20$　$5 \times 5 = 25$ . . .

Each product (0, 5, 10, 15, 20, 25) is a multiple of 5.

What are the next two multiples of 5? _____, _____

A number that is a multiple of two or more numbers is a **common multiple**. Zero is *not* included as a common multiple.

Example

The multiples of 2 are 0, 2, 4, 6, 8, **10**, 12, 14, 16, 18, **20**, . . .

The multiples of 5 are 0, 5, **10**, 15, **20**, 25, 30, 35, . . .

The numbers 10 and 20 are multiples of both 5 and 2. Therefore, 10 and 20 are common multiples of 5 and 2.

What are the next two common multiples of 5 and 2? _____, _____

The least of the common multiples is called the **least common multiple** or **LCM**. The least common multiple (the smaller multiple) of 5 and 2 is 10. (Remember, zero is not included as a common multiple.)

Common Factors

A number that divides another number exactly (with no remainder) is a factor of that number.

Examples

▶

A. What numbers divide 16 exactly?

$16 \div \mathbf{1} = 16$

$16 \div \mathbf{2} = 8$

$16 \div \mathbf{4} = 4$

$16 \div \mathbf{8} = 2$

$16 \div \mathbf{16} = 1$

B. What numbers divide 20 exactly?

$20 \div \mathbf{1} = 20$

$20 \div \mathbf{2} = 10$

$20 \div \mathbf{4} = 5$

$20 \div \mathbf{5} = 4$

$20 \div \mathbf{10} = 2$

$20 \div \mathbf{20} = 1$

The **common factors** of 16 and 20 are 1, 2, and 4. Since 4 is the greatest of the common factors, it is the **greatest common factor** (**GCF**) of 16 and 20.

☰ PRACTICE

Directions: Fill in the two missing multiples for each number.

1. Multiples of 4: 0, _____, 8, _____, 16, 20, 24, . . .

   Multiples of 6: 0, 6, 12, 18, _____, _____, . . .

   Multiples of 8: 0, 8, 16, _____, _____, 40, . . .

   Multiples of 9: 0, 9, 18, _____, 36, _____, . . .

2. What is the least common multiple of 6 and 8? _____

   What are the first two common multiples of 6 and 9? _____, _____

Directions: List the factors for each number.

3. Factors of 7: _____

   Factors of 10: _____

   Factors of 14: _____

   Factors of 21: _____

4. What are the common factors of 7 and 14? _____, _____

   What is the greatest common factor of 14 and 21? _____

Prime and Composite Numbers

Some whole numbers have only two factors—the number itself and the number 1. These are called **prime numbers**.

 Example

▶ 2, 3, and 5 are prime numbers.

$2 = 2 \times 1$ $3 = 3 \times 1$ $5 = 5 \times 1$

4 is not a prime number.

$4 = 4 \times 1$ $4 = 2 \times 2$

4 is a **composite number** (a number with *more* than two factors).

Is 6 a prime number or a composite number? _____

Is 7 a prime number or a composite number? _____

Is 9 a prime number or a composite number? _____

 0 and 1 are neither prime nor composite numbers.

Prime factorization is a way to express a composite number by using two or more prime numbers.

For example, 9 is a composite number. The expression 3×3 is the prime factorization of 9. It shows the value of 9 by using only prime numbers.

Factor trees can help you determine the prime factorization of a number.

≣ Example

▶ Look at the factor tree for 24, shown at the right.

To make a factor tree, begin by writing the number (24). Then write two of its factors underneath (6 and 4). Keep writing the factors of each number until you have only prime numbers at the bottom of the tree.

The prime factorization of 24 also can be expressed using exponents: $2^3 \times 3$.

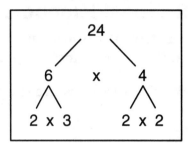

≣ PRACTICE

Directions: Complete the following problems.

1. Draw a factor tree for 120.

2. Draw a factor tree for 45.

Express 120 using exponents.

Express 45 using exponents.

_____

_____

Lesson 3: Ordering Numbers

This lesson will review how to order several different types of numbers.

Rational Numbers

A **rational number** is a number that can be expressed in the form $\frac{a}{b}$ where a and b are both integers and b is *not* equal to zero.

Whole numbers are the set of natural numbers and zero:

$$\{0, 1, 2, 3, 4, \ldots\}$$

Integers are the set of numbers consisting of whole numbers and their opposites:

$$\{\ldots {}^-3, {}^-2, {}^-1, 0, 1, 2, 3, \ldots\}$$

 Zero (0) is neither positive nor negative.

Place Value

When we compare and order rational numbers, it is important to show **place value**. The table below shows the place values for 5,678,126.493.

millions	hundred thousands	ten thousands	thousands	hundreds	tens	ones	decimal point	tenths	hundredths	thousandths
5	6	7	8	1	2	6	•	4	9	3

Ordering and Comparing Decimals

A **decimal** is a number form that expresses a whole as divided into ten equal parts (tenths), one hundred equal parts (hundredths), and so on.

To put decimals in order, compare their place values.

 **Example**

► Which of the following numbers has the greatest value?

714.35923   714.866   714.87   714.1223

It is easier to compare these numbers if you line up their decimal points.

		tenths	hundredths	thousandths	ten thousandths	hundred thousandths
A.	714 .	3	5	9	2	3
B.	714 .	8	6	6		
C.	714 .	8	7			
D.	714 .	1	2	2	3	

Compare the whole numbers (to the left of the decimal point) first. Since all of them are the same, look at the numbers to the right of the decimal point, in the tenths place. Notice that 8 is the largest value in the tenths column. However, both B and C have an 8 in the tenths place. You'll need to move one more decimal place to the right, to compare the hundredths place. Which number has the greatest value?

Choice C, 714.87, has the greatest value.

 **PRACTICE**

Directions: Complete the following problems.

1. Circle the decimal that has the *greatest* value.

   2.39183   2.53605   2.9122   2.2239   2.39299

2. Circle the decimal that has the *least* value.

   1.12336   1.78643   1.456745   1.47   1.6587

3. Rewrite the following decimals in order from *greatest* to *least*.

   6.2349   6.25   6.70333   6.098   6.465

Ordering and Comparing Fractions

A **fraction** is a way of expressing parts of a whole.

$$\dfrac{4}{5} \begin{array}{l} \rightarrow \text{numerator} \\ \rightarrow \text{denominator} \end{array}$$

The fraction $\frac{4}{5}$ means 4 parts of a whole that is divided into 5 equal parts, as shown below.

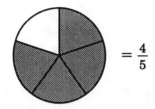 $= \frac{4}{5}$

Fractions also can be combined with integers to form **mixed numbers**. For example, $2\frac{7}{8}$ is a mixed number.

Fractions can be compared more easily if they have a **common denominator**. Two or more fractions have a common denominator when their denominators are the same.

**Example**

 $\frac{3}{5}$ and $\frac{1}{5}$ have a common denominator of 5.

Since the two fractions have a common denominator, you can compare them directly.

$$\frac{3}{5} > \frac{1}{5}$$

> is greater than
< is less than

It's hard to compare the following fractions because their denominators are all different.

$$\frac{2}{3} \qquad \frac{5}{6} \qquad \frac{15}{24}$$

 **Example**

▶ To change these fractions so they have a common denominator, find the **least common multiple** of the denominators. The least common multiple is the smallest number that can be divided evenly by all the denominators.

The smallest number that can be divided evenly by 3, 6, and 24 is 24.

$$24 \div \mathbf{3} = \mathbf{8} \qquad 24 \div \mathbf{6} = \mathbf{4} \qquad 24 \div \mathbf{24} = \mathbf{1}$$

3, 4, 6, 8, and 24 are all **factors** of 24. To change the fractions so that they have a common denominator, multiply both the numerator and the denominator by the appropriate factors.

Multiply the 2 and 3 in $\frac{2}{3}$ by 8: $\frac{2 \times 8}{3 \times 8} = \frac{16}{24}$

Multiply the 5 and 6 in $\frac{5}{6}$ by 4: $\frac{5 \times 4}{6 \times 4} = \frac{20}{24}$

$\frac{15}{24}$ already has the common denominator of 24.

Once the fractions have a common denominator, it is much easier to compare them.

$\frac{2}{3}$	$\frac{5}{6}$	$\frac{15}{24}$
becomes	becomes	remains
↓	↓	↓
$\frac{16}{24}$	$\frac{20}{24}$	$\frac{15}{24}$

Now it's easy to put them in order from least to greatest.

$\frac{15}{24}$	$\frac{16}{24}$	$\frac{20}{24}$
$\frac{15}{24}$	$\left(\frac{2}{3}\right)$	$\left(\frac{5}{6}\right)$

You also can convert fractions to decimals and then compare them.

Example

▶ Order the following fractions from least to greatest.

$$\frac{8}{19} \qquad\qquad \frac{15}{22} \qquad\qquad \frac{19}{37}$$

Change the fractions to decimals by dividing the numerator by the denominator and then compare the decimals.

$$\frac{8}{19} = 8 \div 19 = 0.421$$

$$\frac{15}{22} = 15 \div 22 = 0.618$$

$$\frac{19}{37} = 19 \div 37 = 0.514$$

Putting the fractions in order is much easier now.

$\frac{8}{19}$	$\frac{19}{37}$	$\frac{15}{22}$
becomes	becomes	remains
↓	↓	↓
(0.421)	(0.514)	(0.618)

PRACTICE

Directions: Complete the following problems.

1. Circle the fraction that has the *greatest* value.

$$\frac{4}{5} \qquad\qquad \frac{17}{20} \qquad\qquad \frac{23}{40}$$

2. Circle the fraction that has the *least* value.

$$\frac{3}{16} \qquad\qquad \frac{5}{8} \qquad\qquad \frac{1}{4}$$

3. Rewrite the following fractions in order from *least* to *greatest*.

$$\frac{4}{18} \qquad\qquad \frac{5}{6} \qquad\qquad \frac{2}{3}$$

Ordering and Comparing Integers, Decimals, and Fractions

When you want to put a combination of integers, decimals, and/or fractions in order, it helps to convert from one form to another so that comparisons are easier to make.

≣ Example

▶ Order the following numbers from least to greatest.

$$3 \qquad \frac{15}{4} \qquad 3.0075 \qquad \frac{9}{5}$$

Below is an one way to make comparisons between the numbers more easily.

Change $\frac{15}{4}$ to a mixed number: $\frac{15}{4} = 3\frac{3}{4}$

Change $\frac{9}{5}$ to a mixed number: $\frac{9}{5} = 1\frac{4}{5}$

3	$\frac{15}{4}$	3.0075	$\frac{9}{5}$
remains	becomes	remains	becomes
↓	↓	↓	↓
3	$3\frac{3}{4}$	3.0075	$1\frac{4}{5}$

If you're still not sure how to order 3.0075 and $3\frac{3}{4}$, try converting $3\frac{3}{4}$ to a decimal: $3\frac{3}{4} = 3.75$

Now you're ready to order the numbers from least to greatest.

$$\frac{9}{5} \qquad 3 \qquad 3.0075 \qquad \frac{15}{4}$$

$$\left(1\frac{4}{5}\right) \qquad\qquad\qquad \left(3\frac{3}{4} \text{ or } 3.75\right)$$

Another way numbers can be ordered is on a **number line**.

≣ Example

▶ If you were to place 0.12 on this number line, where would you put it?

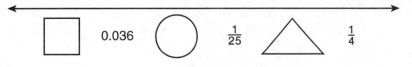

Just as you did with combinations of integers, fractions, and decimals, converting some of the numbers to another form makes this problem easier.

Change $\frac{1}{4}$ to a decimal: $\frac{1}{4} = 0.25$

(0.12 is smaller than 0.25, so 0.12 would be to the left of $\frac{1}{4}$ on the line.)

Change $\frac{1}{25}$ to a decimal: $\frac{1}{25} = 0.04$

Now you can place 0.12 in its proper place on the number line.

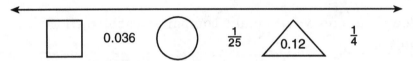

 **PRACTICE**

Directions: Complete the following problems.

1. Order the following numbers from *least* to *greatest*.

   $\frac{26}{3}$ 13.87671 $\frac{15}{2}$ 7.02

   _____

2. Order the following numbers from *least* to *greatest*.

   0.03 $\frac{1}{8}$ 0.0087 $\frac{7}{32}$

   _____

3. Where should 0.394 be placed on the number line?

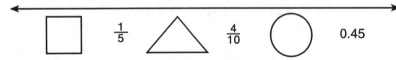

☰ Put Your Skills to the Test

1. What is the equivalent of 125?
   A. 3^5
   B. 5^3
   C. 25×25
   D. 5×10^3

2. The sales tax in a town is 8%. What fraction of a product purchased does that represent?
   A. $\frac{8}{10}$
   B. $\frac{4}{5}$
   C. $\frac{8}{100}$
   D. $\frac{80}{100}$

3. Sasha earns a 4% commission on every piece of stereo equipment she sells. Which expression below correctly shows the way to calculate Sasha's commission on a jam box priced at $89.99?
   A. 89.99×0.4
   B. $89.99 + 4$
   C. 89.99×0.04
   D. $89.99 \times \frac{4}{10}$

4. Which number has common factors of 5, 8, and 10?
   A. 25
   B. 40
   C. 45
   D. 50

5. Which of the following groups of decimals is in order from *least* to *greatest*, reading from left to right?

A. 5.5876	5.5	5.429	5.898	5.17
B. 5.5	5.5876	5.898	5.429	5.17
C. 5.17	5.5	5.5876	5.429	5.898
D. 5.17	5.429	5.5	5.5876	5.898

6. Four people worked together to collect cans for their school's aluminum can drive. Robert collected $\frac{1}{8}$ of the total amount brought in by the group, Steven collected 0.35 of the total, Marie collected 0.15 of the total, and Ellen collected $\frac{6}{16}$ of the total. Which person collected the *smallest amount*?
   A. Robert
   B. Steven
   C. Marie
   D. Ellen

7. A certain type of machine part must be no smaller than 0.7 inch and no larger than $\frac{7}{8}$ of an inch wide. A part measuring $\frac{11}{16}$ of an inch wide is —

 A. 0.0125 inch too small.   C. 0.125 inch too small.
 B. 0.0125 inch too large.   D. 0.125 inch too large.

8. Last year the swim club raised $30 through its fund-raising activities. This year its goal is to raise 350% of last year's figure. If the club reaches its goal, how much money will it raise?

Show your work.

Answer: _____

9. Andrea was measuring the lengths of different insects for her biology class. Her specimens were $\frac{3}{4}$ inch, $\frac{5}{10}$ inch, $\frac{1}{6}$ inch, and $\frac{3}{5}$ inch long. Which was the *longest*?

Show your work.

Answer:_____

10. The area of the earth's largest ocean, the Pacific, is about 181,000,000 square kilometers. The area of the earth's smallest ocean, the Arctic, is about 14,000,000 square kilometers.

Part A

How much greater is the area of the Pacific Ocean than that of the Arctic Ocean?

Show your work.

Answer:_____

Part B

Express the answer in scientific notation.

Answer:_____

unit 2

Operations

Lesson 4: Basic Operations

There are four basic operations in math: addition, subtraction, multiplication, and division.

 Examples

▶ Addition

addends
↓ ↓
$3 + 7 = 10$
↑
sum

$$\begin{array}{r} 3.69 \\ + 5.47 \\ \hline 9.16 \end{array}$$

$$\begin{array}{r} \frac{1}{3} = \frac{5}{15} \\ + \frac{2}{5} = \frac{6}{15} \\ \hline \frac{11}{15} \end{array}$$

$$\begin{array}{r} 2\frac{1}{7} \\ + 4\frac{4}{7} \\ \hline 6\frac{5}{7} \end{array}$$

 Examples

▶ Subtraction

$5 - 4 = 1$
↑
difference

$$\begin{array}{r} 17.89 \\ - 9.47 \\ \hline 8.42 \end{array}$$

$$\begin{array}{r} \frac{4}{9} = \frac{20}{45} \\ - \frac{1}{5} = \frac{9}{45} \\ \hline \frac{11}{45} \end{array}$$

$$\begin{array}{r} 3\frac{4}{5} \\ - 1\frac{2}{5} \\ \hline 2\frac{2}{5} \end{array}$$

Examples

▶ Multiplication

factors
↓ ↓
$4 \times 3 = 12$ ← product

$5.13 \times 2.4 = 12.312$

$\frac{3}{4} \times \frac{2}{7} = \frac{6}{28} = \frac{3}{14}$

$2\frac{2}{5} \times 3\frac{1}{3} = \frac{12}{5} \times \frac{10}{3} = \frac{120}{15} = 8$

Examples

▶ Division

$$\begin{array}{r} \text{quotient} \rightarrow \quad 7 \text{ R}1 \\ \text{divisor} \rightarrow 2 \overline{)15} \leftarrow \text{dividend} \\ -14 \\ \hline \text{remainder} \rightarrow \quad 1 \end{array}$$

$$\begin{array}{r} .36 \\ 25 \overline{)9.00} \\ -75\downarrow \\ \hline 150 \\ -150 \\ \hline 0 \end{array}$$

$$\frac{1}{2} \div \frac{3}{4} = \frac{1}{2} \times \frac{4}{3} = \frac{4}{6} = \frac{2}{3}$$

$$3\frac{3}{4} \div 1\frac{1}{2} = \frac{15}{4} \div \frac{3}{2} = \frac{15}{4} \times \frac{2}{3} = \frac{30}{12} = \frac{5}{2} = 2\frac{1}{2}$$

 PRACTICE

Directions: Complete the following problems.

1. $\frac{3}{5} - \frac{2}{6} =$ _____

2. $\frac{4}{5} + \frac{5}{8} =$ _____

3. $\frac{1}{5} \times \frac{3}{4} =$ _____

4. $7 \times \frac{1}{4} =$ _____

5. $\frac{3}{7} \div \frac{4}{5} =$ _____

6. $2\frac{4}{5} \div 10 =$ _____

7. $5 - 3.2 =$ _____

8. $5 + 0.32 + 7.193 =$ _____

9. $7.53 \times 0.95 =$ _____

10. $35.28 \div 6.3 =$ _____

Addition and Subtraction of Integers

- The sum of positive integers is positive: $47 + 22 = 69$
- The sum of negative integers is negative: $^-17 + ^-22 = ^-39$
- The sum of positive and negative integers will have the sign of the **number** with the greater absolute value.

$$^-11 + 6 = ^-5$$
$$13 + ^-9 = 4$$

The **absolute value** of a number is the distance a number is from zero. The symbol $|n|$ is used to show absolute value.

 Example

▶ The absolute value of $9 = |9| = 9$

The absolute value of $^-9 = |^-9| = 9$

Look at the number line below.

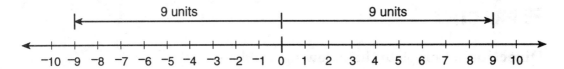

The distance from $^-9$ to 0 is 9 units. The distance from 9 to 0 is also 9 units.

- When subtracting an integer, add its opposite:

$$^-8 - ^-4 =$$
$$^-8 + 4 = ^-4$$

$$9 - 5 =$$
$$9 + ^-5 = 4$$

Multiplication and Division of Integers

- The product or quotient of two positive integers is positive.

$$7 \times 7 = 49 \qquad (+) \times (+) = (+)$$

$$16 \div 4 = 4 \qquad (+) \div (+) = (+)$$

- The product or quotient of two negative integers is positive.

$$^-4 \times {}^-5 = 20 \qquad (-) \times (-) = (+)$$

$$^-14 \div {}^-2 = 7 \qquad (-) \div (-) = (+)$$

- The product or quotient of one negative and one positive integer is negative.

$$3 \times {}^-4 = {}^-12 \qquad (+) \times (-) = (-)$$

$$^-30 \div 6 = {}^-5 \qquad (-) \div (+) = (-)$$

PRACTICE

Directions: Complete the following problems.

1. $19 + {}^-8 = $ ___-11___

2. $^-15 + {}^-15 = $ ___-30___

3. $^-63 - 34 = $ ___-97___

4. $228 \div {}^-12 = $ ___-19___

5. $^-48 \div {}^-4 = $ ___+12___

6. $8 \times {}^-10 = $ ___-80___

Lesson 5: Roots and Powers

This lesson explores the relationship between roots and powers.

Numbers Expressed as Radicals

$\sqrt{\ }$ is called a **radical**. It is used to indicate a square root.

 **Example**

▶ $\sqrt{16}$ means "the square root of 16."

$\sqrt{16} = 4$

$4^2 = 4 \times 4 = 16$

$(^-4)^2 = {}^-4 \times {}^-4 = 16$

> $\sqrt[3]{8}$ means "the cube root of 8"
>
> $\sqrt[3]{8} = 2$
>
> $2 \times 2 \times 2 = 2^3 = 8$

Numbers such as 1, 4, 9, 16, 25, and so on are called **perfect squares** because their square roots are rational numbers. Perfect squares and their square roots are both rational numbers.

$\sqrt{2}$, $\sqrt{3}$, $\sqrt{5}$, and so on are **irrational numbers**. They are not perfect squares. The square root of numbers that are not perfect squares have decimals that do not terminate or repeat.

Example

▶ Find $\sqrt{2}$.

There is no rational number that can be multiplied by itself to get the number 2. However, we know that the square root of 2 must be greater than 1 (because $1 \times 1 = 1$) and less than 2 (because $2 \times 2 = 4$).

The calculator shows $\sqrt{2}$ as 1.414213562. . . . This is a non-terminating decimal, and there is no repeating cycle of digits.

Therefore, $\sqrt{2}$ is an irrational number.

How to Find Square Roots

The fastest way to find square roots is by using a calculator with the $\sqrt{}$ key. If your calculator does not have this key, you can always multiply two equal factors until you find an approximate answer.

Estimating square roots

When you do not know the exact square root of a number, or if you do not have a calculator, you can estimate the square root.

 **Example**

▶ Find $\sqrt{33}$.

Step 1: **Place the number between the closest perfect squares.**

33 is between the perfect squares of 25 and 36.

Step 2: **Find the square roots of the perfect squares.**

What are the square roots of 25 and 36? 5 and 6

Step 3: **Estimate the square root of the original number** using the information in Step 2.

33 is between 25 and 36, so $\sqrt{33}$ is greater than 5 and less than 6.

(The calculator shows that $\sqrt{33}$ is 5.744562646. . .)

 **PRACTICE**

Directions: Find the square root of each number to two decimal places. (First estimate the square root, then use your calculator.)

1. $\sqrt{81}$ _____12_____

2. $\sqrt{50}$ _____

3. $\sqrt{125}$ _____

4. $\sqrt{144}$ _____

Lesson 6: Order of Operations and Problem Solving

This lesson shows how to use grouping symbols to clarify the intended order of operations.

Order of Operations

When more than one operation is required to solve a problem, you must follow a certain order of operations.

1. If any computations are grouped in parentheses, work them first.
2. Simplify expressions with exponents.
3. Do any multiplication and division in order, from left to right.
4. Do any addition and subtraction in order, from left to right.

It is important to follow the order of operations, as you will see in the example below.

 Example

▶ Russell and Tasha both attempted to solve the following problem:

$$7 + 4 \times 5 = ?$$

Russell got an answer of 55. Tasha got an answer of 27. Who was correct?

Check the order of operations. Since there are no parentheses or exponents, the first step in solving this problem should be multiplication.

$$7 + 4 \times 5 = ?$$
$$4 \times 5 = 20$$

The next step, according to the order of operations, should be addition.

$$7 + 20 = 27$$

Tasha got it right.

Inverse operations

Inverse operations are math operations that are opposites of one another. Addition is the inverse operation of subtraction, and subtraction is the inverse operation of addition. Inverse operations can be very helpful in solving math problems.

Example

$44 + n = 73$

To find n, use the inverse operation of addition, which is subtraction.

Subtract 44 from both sides of the equation.

$$44 - 44 + n = 73 - 44$$
$$0 + n = 29$$
$$n = 29$$

Check your work by replacing n with your answer.

$$44 + \boldsymbol{n} = 73$$
$$44 + \boldsymbol{29} = 73$$

Example

$n - 32 = 19$

To find n, use the inverse operation of subtraction, which is addition.

Add 32 to both sides of the equation.

$$n - 32 + 32 = 19 + 32$$
$$n - 0 = 51$$
$$n = 51$$

Check your work by replacing n with your answer.

$$\boldsymbol{n} - 32 = 19$$
$$\boldsymbol{51} - 32 = 19$$

Multiplication is the inverse operation of division, and division is the inverse operation of multiplication.

≣ Example

▶ $6 \times n = 42$

Use the inverse of multiplication—division.

$$\frac{\cancel{6} \times n}{\cancel{6}} = \frac{42}{6}$$

$$n = 7$$

Be sure to check your work by replacing n with your answer.

$$6 \times \boldsymbol{n} = 42$$

$$6 \times \boldsymbol{7} = 42$$

≣ Example

▶ $\frac{n}{8} = 4$

Use the inverse of division—multiplication.

$$\cancel{8} \times \frac{n}{\cancel{8}} = 4 \times 8$$

$$n = 32$$

Check your work by replacing n with your answer.

$$\frac{n}{8} = 4$$

$$\frac{\boldsymbol{32}}{8} = 4$$

PEMDAS

≡ PRACTICE

Directions: For problems 1–3, identify the order of operations and then find the answer.

1. $3 + 4 \times 2 - 1 =$ _4×2 +3 −1_ _10_

2. $25 - 5 \div 1 + (4.5 - 3) =$ _(4.5−3) 5÷1 −25_ _21.5_

3. $12 + (36 \div 4)^2 \times 3 =$ _36÷4² × 3 +12_ _263._

4. Tough-Stuff Furniture Company makes an average of 353 folding chairs every month. In 12 months, how many folding chairs will the company produce?

_4236_

$$\begin{array}{r} 353 \\ \times\ 12 \\ \hline 706 \\ 353 \\ \hline 4236 \end{array}$$

5. Terry had 239 stamps. James gave him 177 more stamps. Terry wants to put an equal number of stamps on each page in his stamp collecting book. How many stamps could Terry put on 8 pages of the stamp book?

_52_

$$\begin{array}{r} 239 \\ +\ 177 \\ \hline 416 \end{array}$$

$$8\ \overline{)416} \quad \begin{array}{r} 52 \\ 400 \\ \hline 16 \end{array}$$

Problem-Solving Strategies

A variety of strategies can be used to solve math word problems.

Working step-by-step

This step-by-step method will help you understand math problems and make decisions about which operations to use. It will also help you see whether you need to use more than one strategy.

Step 1: Take time to study the problem.

Step 2: Evaluate the information given.

Step 3: Select a strategy for solving the problem.

Step 4: Set up the problem and estimate a reasonable answer.

Step 5: Do the math and check your answer.

Strategies

Problem-solving strategies help you select a **plan** to solve a problem. Examples of problem-solving strategies include:

- Choose an operation—addition, subtraction, multiplication, or division.
- Find a pattern.
- Make a table or organize a list.
- Write an equation.
- Use logical thinking.
- Guess and check.
- Work backwards.
- Solve a simpler problem. (For example, when you have a problem with more than one operation, you break the problem into parts.)
- Visualize the problem. (For example, draw a picture.)

 Example

Last week Ana earned $25 from her paper route. On Saturday, she earned $5.00 for taking care of her neighbors' dogs, which was three dollars more than they usually pay her. Ana always puts 40% of what she earns each week in the bank. After putting away her savings, she spent $\frac{1}{3}$ of what was left at the movies. How much spending money does Ana have left after going to the movies?

Step 1: **Take time to study the problem**. Try to understand or visualize the situation.

What is the problem asking?

How much money does Ana have left after going to the movies?

What information does the problem give?

Ana earned $25 from her paper route and $5 for taking care of the dogs.

This time she earned $3 more than usual.

She saves 40% of her weekly earnings.

Of the money left, she spent $\frac{1}{3}$ at the movies.

Step 2: **Evaluate the information given**. Determine whether or not you need all the information that is given, or if there is information missing.

"Earning $3 more than usual" is extra information that is not needed to solve the problem.

Step 3: **Select a strategy for solving the problem.** Read the problem again and try to determine what operations or strategies will solve the problem.

Look back at the information given. In order to solve the problem, you will probably have to add, multiply or divide, and subtract.

Since Ana earned money on two different occasions, you know that you will need to **add** to get the total of what she earned.

To find a dollar amount for the percent of money she saves, you will either **multiply** or set up a proportion.

To find the amount left, **subtract** the money she saves from the total that she earned.

To find how much she spent at the movies, you will either **multiply** by $\frac{1}{3}$ or **divide** by 3.

Finally, you have to use **subtraction** to find out how much spending money Ana has left.

Step 4: **Set up the problem and estimate a reasonable answer.**

25 + 5 = total earned

She saved 40%.

Total earned × 0.40 = amount saved

Total earned − amount saved = money left before the movies.

Of the money left, she spent $\frac{1}{3}$ at the movies.

$\frac{1}{3}$ of the money left = ?

You can quickly estimate that Ana will have less than half of her original earnings left for spending money.

Step 5: **Do the math and check your answer.** Do the computations needed to solve the problem.

25 + 5 = 30	Ana earned $30.
30 × 0.40 = 12	Ana saved $12.
30 − 12 = 18	She had $18 left.
$\frac{1}{3}$ of 18 = 6	She spent $6 at the movies.

How much spending money does Ana have left after going to the movies?

18 − 6 = 12	Ana has $12 left after going to the movies.

Check the correctness of your answer. Make sure all of Ana's money is accounted for. Then ask yourself, "Is my answer reasonable? Does it make sense?"

≡ PRACTICE

Directions: Identify a problem-solving strategy or strategies that will help you solve this problem.

1. The first $10,000 Joshua earns is not taxed by the federal government. For every additional dollar after $10,000, Joshua is taxed 35%. If he earns $25,000, how much will he have after taxes?

   Strategy:_____

   Solve the problem using the strategy you have selected.

   $19,500

Estimation

Step 4 of the step-by-step method tells you to "Set up the problem and estimate a reasonable answer." Estimation helps us to make sure our answer is reasonable.

Rounding is a good estimation technique. When rounding whole numbers or decimals, it is important to know place value.

The table below shows place values for the number 13,847.652.

Ten Thousands	Thousands	Hundreds	Tens	Ones	Decimal Point	Tenths	Hundredths	Thousandths
1	3	8	4	7	.	6	5	2

When rounding, follow these instructions:

- Look at the digit to the **right** of the place to which you are rounding.
- If the digit is **5 or more**, increase the digit in the place you are rounding by one.
- If the digit is **less than 5**, leave the digit in the place you are rounding the same.

 Example

▶ The whole number represented below is 2,478.

Thousands	Hundreds	Tens	Ones
2	4	7	8

2,478 rounded to the nearest 10 is 2,480   (increase)

2,478 rounded to the nearest 100 is 2,500   (increase)

2,478 rounded to the nearest 1,000 is 2,000   (leave the same)

Example

▶ The decimal number represented below is 3.428.

Ones		Tenths	Hundredths	Thousandths
3	.	4	2	8

3.428 rounded to the nearest one is 3   (leave the same)

3.428 rounded to the nearest tenth is 3.4   (leave the same)

3.428 rounded to the nearest hundredth is 3.43   (increase)

≡ PRACTICE

Directions: Round 1,843.746 to the nearest . . .

1. ten _____1840_____

2. hundred _____1800_____

3. thousand _____2000_____

4. whole number _____1,844_____

5. tenth _____1843.7_____

6. hundredth _____1843.75_____

Directions: Solve the following problem.

7. Erin wanted to spend 5 hours a week studying. The table below shows the time she spent studying. *Estimate* how many more hours she would have needed to study to have reached 5 hours.

Monday	Tuesday	Wednesday	Thursday	Weekend (Fri., Sat., Sun.)
55 min	$1\frac{1}{2}$ hr	25 min	35 min	$\frac{1}{4}$ hr

_____1¼ hrs._____

On the lines below, show or explain how you estimated your answer.

_____

_____

_____

Rounding Fractions and Mixed Numbers

If the fraction is $\frac{1}{2}$ **or greater, round up to 1** (or to the next whole number in a mixed number).

$1\frac{3}{4}$ rounded to the nearest whole number is 2.

If the fraction is **less than $\frac{1}{2}$, round down** by dropping the fraction.

$3\frac{2}{7}$ rounded to the nearest whole number is 3.

Example of Visual Representation: Venn Diagrams

Venn diagrams help us see relationships among numbers, people, animals, plants—almost anything that you can put into a group.

Example

At Washington Middle School, a total of 28 students play soccer, basketball, and/or volleyball. Of these students, 20 play soccer, 10 play basketball, and 15 play volleyball; 7 play both soccer and basketball, 9 play both soccer and volleyball, 5 play both basketball and volleyball, and 4 play all three sports. How many of the students play *only* soccer, basketball, or volleyball?

Let's see how problem-solving strategies help us solve this problem.

Step 1: **Take time to study the problem.** Try to understand or visualize the situation. What is the problem asking?

How many of the students play *only* soccer, basketball, or volleyball?

In other words, the problem asks you to tell how many students play only one of the sports mentioned.

What information does the problem give you? Making a list will help you organize the information. Complete the following list.

20 students play soccer

__10__ students play basketball

__15__ students play volleyball

7 students play soccer and basketball

__9__ students play soccer and volleyball

__5__ students play basketball and volleyball

4 students play all three (soccer, basketball, and volleyball)

The total number of students playing soccer, basketball, and/or volleyball is 28.

(By now you must have suspected that a diagram or drawing will help you visualize the situation.)

Step 2: **Evaluate the information given.** Determine whether or not you need all the information that is given, or if there is information missing.

You have all the necessary information.

Step 3: **Select a strategy for solving the problem.**

The best strategy for solving this problem is to visualize the problem. A Venn diagram will help you do this. You will probably need to use two operations: addition and subtraction.

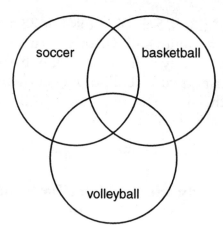

Step 4: **Set up the problem and estimate a reasonable answer.**

The list we made in Step 1 will help us set up the problem.

Using this list we can estimate that the number of students who play *only* soccer has to be less than 20, the number of students who play *only* basketball has to be less than 10, and the number of students who play *only* volleyball has to be less than 15.

Step 5: **Do the math and check your answer.** Do the computations needed to solve the problem.

Look at the diagram. The section in which the three circles overlap indicates where we should place the 4 students who play all three sports.

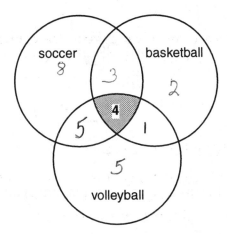

How many students play both soccer and basketball?

_____7_____

Look at the section that is shared by both circles (where the circles for soccer and basketball overlap). Since part of the overlapping section already has 4 students, we subtract that number from 7.

$$7 - 4 = 3$$

Write 3 where it belongs in the diagram.

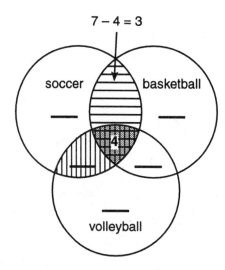

7 − 4 = 3

How many students play both soccer and volleyball?

_____

The section that is shared by both circles already has 4 students, therefore, 9 − 4 = 5. Write 5 in the section where it belongs in the diagram.

With this information in the diagram, we can now find how many students play *only* soccer.

In the circle that shows the students who play soccer, you have already placed 3, 4, and 5 students. To find the number of students who play *only* soccer, subtract from 20.

20 − 3 − 4 − 5 = 8

Of the 20 students who play soccer, 8 play *only* soccer. Write the number 8 where it belongs in the diagram.

Use the same process to find how many students play *only* basketball and how many students play *only* volleyball. Complete the diagram above.

Check your answer.

Add the number of students in the circles. If you do not have 20 students playing soccer, 15 playing volleyball, and 10 playing basketball, go back and check your work.

Show your computation here.

PRACTICE

Directions: Look at the diagram below. Which of the following statements are false and which are true? Write F if the statement is false and T if the statement is true.

➡ When parts of the circles overlap, it means that members of those groups share a certain characteristic. When circles do not overlap, it means that group members do not share that characteristic.

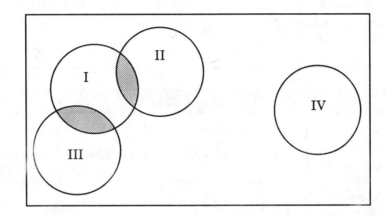

1. <u>All members</u> of group I are members of groups II and III.   _F_

2. Some members of group I are members of groups II and III.   _T_

3. No members of group IV are members of group I.   _T_

4. Some members of group III are members of group II.   _F_

5. <u>All members</u> of group I are members of group III.   _F_

6. Some members of group II are members of group III.   _F_

7. Some members of group I are members of group II.   _T_

on 7: Number Properties

...son gives you a chart that explains how number properties are related to the basic operations.

Number Properties

Study

Commutative Property		
The *order* of the numbers (addends or factors) does not change the sum or the product.	**Addition** $a + b = b + a$ $3 + 4 = 4 + 3$ $7 = 7$	**Multiplication** $a \cdot b = b \cdot a$ $2 \times 5 = 5 \times 2$ $10 = 10$

Associative Property		
The *grouping* of the numbers does not change the sum or the product.	**Addition** $(a + b) + c = a + (b + c)$ $(5 + 3) + 2 = 5 + (3 + 2)$ $8 + 2 = 5 + 5$ $10 = 10$	**Multiplication** $(a \cdot b) \cdot c = a \cdot (b \cdot c)$ $(2 \times 4) \times 3 = 2 \times (4 \times 3)$ $8 \times 3 = 2 \times 12$ $24 = 24$

Distributive Property	
This property relates the operations of addition and multiplication.	$a(b + c) = (a \cdot b) + (a \cdot c)$ $3(5 + 7) = (3 \times 5) + (3 \times 7)$ $3 (12) = 15 + 21$ $36 = 36$

Other Properties	
A number added to zero will be equal to that same number.	**Identity for Addition** $a + 0 = a$ $198 + 0 = 198$
A number multiplied by one will be equal to that same number.	**Identity for Multiplication** $a \cdot 1 = a$ $43 \times 1 = 43$
A number multiplied by zero will be equal to zero.	**Zero Product Property** $a \cdot 0 = 0$ $1{,}287 \times 0 = 0$
A number added to its opposite will be equal to zero.	**Inverse for Addition** $a + {}^{-}a = 0$ $8 + {}^{-}8 = 0$
A number multiplied by its reciprocal will be equal to one.	**Inverse for Multiplication** $\dfrac{a}{b} \cdot \dfrac{b}{a} = 1$ $\dfrac{2}{3} \times \dfrac{3}{2} = 1$

PRACTICE

Directions: Identify the number property shown in questions 1 and 2.

1. $10 + 0 = 10$ _identity for addition_

2. $7(3 + 5) = (7 \times 3) + (7 \times 5)$ _distributive property_

3. Use words and/or numbers to explain why there is no commutative property for subtraction and division.

   $5 - 3 \neq 3 \cdot 5$

   $2 \neq {}^{-}2$

4. Give an example of the identity for multiplication.

   $7 - 1 = 7$

5. Give an example of the associative property of addition.

   $(3+4) + 5 = 3(4+5)$

Lesson 8: Ratio and Proportion

A **ratio** is a comparison of two numbers, usually expressed as a fraction.

 Example

▶ At the Science Fair, 6 projects won awards. There were 30 projects submitted. What part of the projects received awards?

You can write this ratio as $\frac{6}{30}$ or, in lowest terms, $\frac{1}{5}$.

What is the ratio of projects that did *not* win awards?

$30 - 6 = 24$

The ratio is $\frac{24}{30}$ or $\frac{4}{5}$.

 Example

▶ Five students from Hoover Junior High submitted projects at the Science Fair. Two received awards. What is the ratio of awards to students?

The ratio is $\frac{2}{5}$ → $\frac{\text{awards}}{\text{students}}$

This means that of 5 students, 2 received awards.

PRACTICE

Directions: Use the information below to answer questions 1 and 2.

A baseball team won 12 games and lost 3.

1. What is the ratio of games won to games lost?

   $\underline{\quad 4 \text{ to } 1 \quad}$

2. What is the ratio of games won to games played?

   $\underline{\quad 12 \text{ to } 15 \quad 4 \text{ to } 5 \quad}$

3. What is the ratio of boys to girls in your classroom?

   $\underline{\quad \frac{6}{4} = \frac{3}{2} \quad}$

4. What is the ratio of 8th-grade teachers to students in your class?

   $\underline{\quad \frac{2}{8} \quad}$

46

Proportion

A **proportion** expresses the relationship between two ratios. It states that the two ratios are equal.

$\frac{2}{5}$ and $\frac{4}{10}$ are equal ratios, therefore $\frac{2}{5} = \frac{4}{10}$ is a proportion.

A proportion has two **cross products**, which are equal to each other. To find them, multiply the numbers located diagonally across from one another. In the proportion $\frac{2}{5} = \frac{4}{10}$, the cross products are 2×10 and 4×5.

$$\frac{2}{5} \diagdown\!\!\!\!\diagup \frac{4}{10}$$

$$2 \times 10 = 20 \qquad 4 \times 5 = 20$$

$$2 \times 10 = 4 \times 5$$

$$20 = 20 \leftarrow \text{The cross products are equal.}$$

Example

The pet store sells a certain kind of fish at a price of 2 for $5. You want to buy 5 fish. How much will 5 fish cost?

Step 1: **Set up a proportion.**

$$\frac{\text{fish}}{\text{dollars}} \rightarrow \frac{2}{5} = \frac{5}{n}$$

Step 2: **Multiply to get cross products.**

$$2 \times n = 5 \times 5$$
$$2 \times n = 25$$

Step 3: **Simplify your equation.** Divide both sides of the equation by 2 so that n stands alone.

$$\frac{2n}{2} = \frac{25}{2} \qquad n = 12.50, \text{ so 5 fish will cost } \$12.50$$

Step 4: **Check your answer.** Make sure that the cross products are equivalent by substituting the answer for n.

$$2 \times \boldsymbol{n} = 25$$
$$2 \times \boldsymbol{12.50} = 25$$
$$25 = 25$$

☰ PRACTICE

Directions: In problems 1–3, solve each proportion for n.

1. $\frac{6}{12} = \frac{n}{50}$ $\underline{25}$

$\frac{6}{12} = \frac{n}{50}$ $2n = 50$ $2 \times \frac{n}{25} = 50$
$\frac{6}{12} = \frac{n}{50}$ $n = 25$

2. $\frac{2}{3} = \frac{n}{100}$ $\underline{66\,\frac{2}{3}}$

$\frac{2}{3} \diagup \frac{n}{100}$ $\frac{3n}{3} = 200$ $n = 66\frac{2}{3}$

3. $\frac{5}{7} = \frac{10}{n}$ $\underline{14}$

$\frac{5}{7} \diagup \frac{10}{n}$ $\frac{5n}{5} = \frac{70}{5}$ $n = 14$

4. At school, colored markers are on sale 3 for 93¢. You want to buy 7. How much money will you spend? Show your work in the space below.

$\underline{\$2.17}$

$\begin{array}{r} 31¢ \\ \times\ 7 \\ \hline \$2.17 \end{array}$

Put Your Skills to the Test

1. What is the correct solution for $(8 \times 5) \div 20 + 5$?

   A. 1.6

   B. 5

   C. 7

   D. 8.2

2. Which of the following expressions is equal to $4(2 + 5)$?

   A. $(4 \times 2) + (4 \times 5)$

   B. $(4 \times 2) \times 5$

   C. $(4 + 5) + (4 + 2)$

   D. $(4 + 2) \times (4 + 5)$

3. Which number is the *greatest*?

   A. $\frac{22}{1}$

   B. $\sqrt{81}$

   C. $20.934356\ldots$

   D. 9^2

4. Four friends each ordered a medium pizza for lunch. After lunch, Jack took home $\frac{1}{3}$ of his pizza, Eleanor took home $0.666\ldots$ of her pizza, Flo took home 25% of her pizza, and Michael took home $\sqrt{1}$. Which of the friends took home the *least* amount of pizza?

   A. Jack

   B. Eleanor

   C. Flo

   D. Michael

5. How would you solve $n - 59 = 106$?

   A. Add 59 to both sides of the equation.

   B. Divide both sides of the equation by 59.

   C. Multiply both sides of the equation by 59.

   D. Subtract 106 from the right side of the equation.

6. What is the solution for the following equation?

   $$\frac{n}{7} = \frac{18}{1}$$

   A. 0.39

   B. $2\frac{4}{7}$

   C. 25

   D. 126

7. The bakery is having a sale on cookies. Kathleen bought 12 for $1. James spent 75¢. How many cookies did James buy?

   A. 6

   B. 8

   C. 9

   D. 10

8. The ratio of girls to boys in the Art Club is 4 to 6. What is this ratio expressed as a percent?

Show your work.

Answer: _____

9. Stephanie is playing a guessing game. She gets 15 points for each correct answer and 10 points for each answer that is partially correct. She loses 20 points for each wrong answer. If Stephanie answered 3 questions right, 4 partially correct, and 2 wrong, how many points did she finish with?

Show your work.

Answer: _____

10. Mr. Saylor wrote the following problem on the board and asked his students to solve it.

$$5 + 8 \times 3 - 2$$

One student got an answer of 37. Another student got an answer of 27.

Part A

Determine the correct answer

Show your work.

Answer: _____

Part B

Explain why the students got different answers.

_____

_____

_____

unit **3**

Modeling/Multiple Representation

Lesson 9: Geometric Concepts

This lesson explores relationships involving points, lines, angles and planes.

Lines and Angles

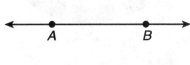

Point: a single location, or position, having no size or dimension

Plane: a flat surface without thickness, extending in all directions

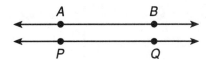

Line: all the points on a never-ending straight path that extends in both directions $\overleftrightarrow{AB}$

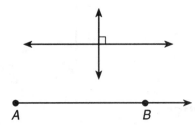

Line segment: all the points on the straight path between two points, including those two points called endpoints $\overline{AB}$

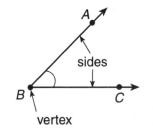

Intersecting lines: lines that meet, or cross

Parallel lines: lines in the same plane that never intersect $\overleftrightarrow{AB} \mid\mid \overleftrightarrow{PQ}$

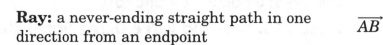

Perpendicular lines: lines that intersect to form right angles (right angles = 90°) $\perp$

Ray: a never-ending straight path in one direction from an endpoint $\overrightarrow{AB}$

An **angle** is formed by two rays that share the same endpoint. The point is called the **vertex**. The rays are called **sides**.

$\angle$ is used to indicate an angle. There are different ways to name an angle:

- by the vertex $\angle B$

- by the letters of the three points that form it $\angle ABC$ or $\angle CBA$ (The middle letter names the vertex.)

- by the number or small letter in its interior $\angle 1$, $\angle x$

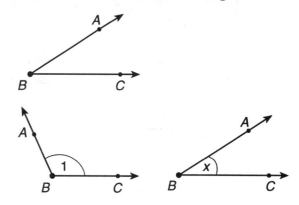

Angles are measured in **degrees** and are given special names according to their measures.

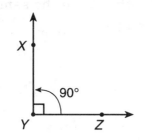

Right angle: has a measure of 90°

The symbol ⌐ is used to indicate a right angle

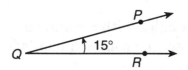

Acute angle: has a measure greater than 0° but less than 90°

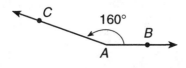

Obtuse angle: has a measure greater than 90° but less than 180°

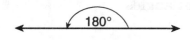

Straight angle: has a measure of 180°; its sides form a straight line

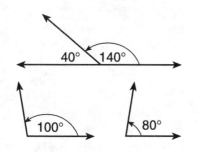

Supplementary angles: two angles whose measures have a sum of 180°

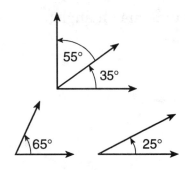

Complementary angles: two angles whose measures have a sum of 90°

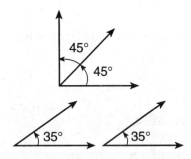

Congruent angles: angles that have the same measure (congruent = the same)

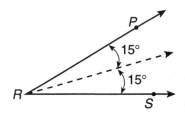

Adjacent angles: two angles with a common side, a common vertex, and no common points within the angles

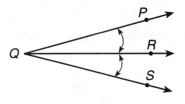

Bisector of an angle: a ray that divides an angle into two congruent angles

© 1999 Buckle Down Publishing Company. DO NOT DUPLICATE.

☰ PRACTICE

Directions: Complete the following problems.

1. Use the figures below to complete the following.

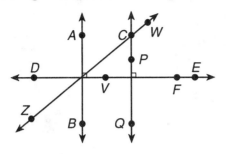   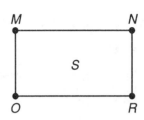

$\overleftrightarrow{AB}$ and $\overleftrightarrow{DE}$ are _____ lines

$\overleftrightarrow{AB}$ and $\overleftrightarrow{PQ}$ are _____ lines

S is a _____ $\overleftrightarrow{DE}$ is a _____

$\overrightarrow{FE}$ is a _____ $\overline{VF}$ is a _____

Name a point: _____

Name perpendicular lines: _____

Name 2 intersecting lines: _____

2. Name the angle and vertex in this figure.

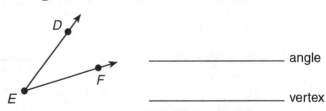

_____ angle

_____ vertex

3. What type of angle is each of the following?

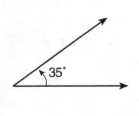   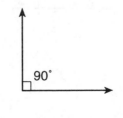   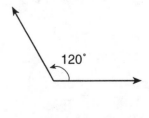

_____   _____   _____

Transversal: a line that intersects two or more lines in the same plane at different points

When parallel lines are cut by a transversal, certain angles are formed.

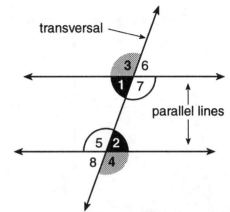

∠1 and ∠2 are **alternate interior** angles.

$m \angle 1 = m \angle 2$ (m = measure)

∠3 and ∠4 are **alternate exterior** angles.

$m \angle 3 = m \angle 4$

∠3 and ∠5 are **corresponding** angles.

$m \angle 3 = m \angle 5$

∠5 and ∠2 are **supplementary** angles.

$m \angle 5 + m \angle 2 = 180°$

 An easy way to remember the relationship among these angles is: When two parallel lines are cut by a transversal, all the large angles are equal and all the small angles are equal.

≣ PRACTICE

Directions: Now use the same figure to list more pairs of:

1. alternate interior angles _____

2. alternate exterior angles _____

3. corresponding angles _____

4. supplementary angles _____

Directions: Use the diagram below to answer the following questions. Lines *h* and *k* are parallel.

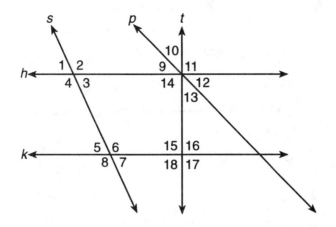

5. If angle 1 is 65°, what is the measure of angle 3? _____

6. If angle 1 is 65°, what is the measure of angle 8? _____

7. If angle 1 is 65°, what is the measure of angle 6? _____

8. If lines *t* and *k* are perpendicular, what is the measure of angle 17?_____

9. If lines *t* and *h* are perpendicular, and if line *p* bisects two of the angles created by lines *h* and *t*, what are the measures of angles 9 and 10?

_____

Measuring Angles

Angles are measured in degrees. To measure the degrees in an angle, you use a **protractor**.

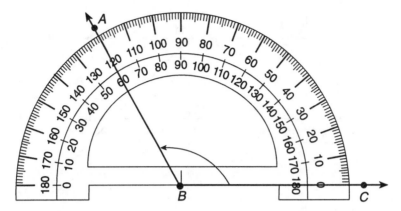

☰ Example

▶ When measuring an angle with a protractor, follow these steps:

Step 1: Place the center of the protractor on the vertex, B, and the base of the protractor on side BC.

Step 2: Read the number of units where side AB passes through the scale.

∠B measures 120°.

The angle was measured starting at the 0 on the right of the protractor, so you read the top row of numbers.

☰ PRACTICE

Directions: Use the protractor shown to measure each angle.

1. ∠*ALB* _____

2. ∠*ALC* _____

3. ∠*ALD* _____

4. ∠*BLD* _____

5. ∠*ALE* _____

6. ∠*ELB* _____

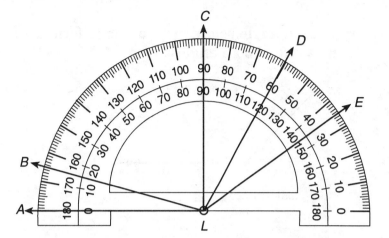

Even if you do not have a protractor, you can still estimate the measure of an angle. Compare the angle in relation to a straight angle and a right angle. Look at the drawing below.

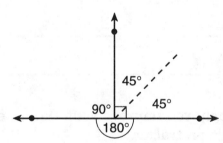

If you start with 180° and cut it in half, you can draw two 90° angles. If you cut 90° in half, you can draw two 45° angles. If you keep cutting each angle in half, you can draw angles of 22.5° and so on.

▤ PRACTICE

Directions: Complete the following problems:

1. In each angle below, draw a line to form a 90° angle, then estimate the measure of both angles.

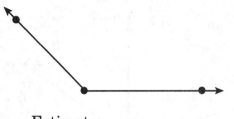

    Estimate: _____   Estimate: _____

2. Measure the angles above with a protractor.

    Measure: _____   Measure: _____

3. How does your estimate compare with the actual measure?

    _____

    _____

 Practice will help you improve your skill in estimating angles without using a protractor.

Lesson 10: Two- and Three-Dimensional S

This lesson introduces you to the visualization and representation of
three-dimensional shapes.

Two-Dimensional Shapes

Two-dimensional shapes are **plane figures**. They have two dimensions: length
and width. Examples of two-dimensional figures are polygons and circles.

Polygons: closed two-dimensional figures formed by line segments or sides. A
polygon is named by its number of sides or angles. For example, a polygon with
3 sides is called a triangle. A polygon with 4 sides is called a quadrilateral.

Triangles: figures with 3 sides and 3 angles. Triangles are named by the
characteristics of their sides and angles.

Scalene Triangle: no congruent sides or congruent angles	**Isosceles Triangle:** two congruent sides and two congruent angles	**Equilateral Triangle:** three congruent sides and three congruent angles
Right Triangle: has a right angle (equals 90°)	**Acute Triangle:** all angles are less than 90°	**Obtuse Triangle:** has an angle that is greater than 90°

 The sum of all the interior angles in any triangle is always
180°.

Quadrilaterals

Quadrilaterals: polygons with 4 sides (line segments).

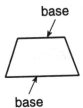

base

base

Trapezoid: a quadrilateral with one pair of parallel sides. The parallel sides are called bases.

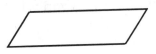

Parallelogram: a quadrilateral in which both pairs of opposite sides are parallel.

Square: a parallelogram with 4 right angles and 4 equal sides.

Rhombus: a parallelogram with 4 equal sides.

Rectangle: a parallelogram with 4 right angles.

Other common polygons

Pentagon: a polygon with 5 sides.

Hexagon: a polygon with 6 sides.

Octagon: a polygon with 8 sides.

Polygons in which all sides and all angles are congruent are called **regular polygons**.

≡ PRACTICE

Directions: Label each letter. Use the term that *most specifically* describes each figure.

1. A _Rhombus_
2. B _parallelogram_
3. C _parallelogram_
4. D _trapezoid_
5. E _rectangle_
6. F _square_
7. G _scalene triangle_

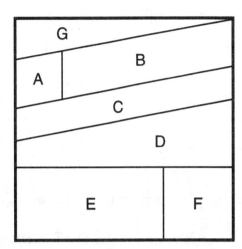

Circles

Circles are closed two-dimensional figures. A **circle** consists of all points in a plane that are an equal distance from a given point called the **center**.

A circle is named by its **center point**. Circle Z is shown below.

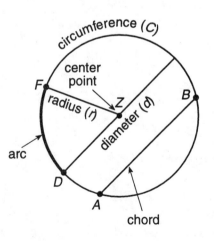

Radius (r): any line segment from the center point to any point on the circle $\left(r = \dfrac{d}{2}\right)$

Diameter (d): a line segment that passes through the center point and has both endpoints on the circle ($d = 2r$)

Chord: a straight line segment that joins two points that lie on the circle

Circumference (C): the distance around the circle ($C = \pi d$ or $C = 2\pi r$)

$\left(\pi = 3.14 \text{ or } \dfrac{22}{7}\right)$

Arc: A portion of a circle between two endpoints on the circle ($\overset{\frown}{DF}$)

≡ PRACTICE

Directions: Complete the following problems:

1. Draw a circle and label all its parts.

2. Explain why a circle is not a polygon.

   _____ not made up of line segements _____

   _____

Three-Dimensional Shapes

The dimensions of a **three-dimensional** figure are its length, width, and height.

The flat surfaces of a three-dimensional figure are called **faces**. The faces intersect to form **edges**, and the endpoint shared by the edges is called a **vertex**.

Here are some examples of three-dimensional figures.

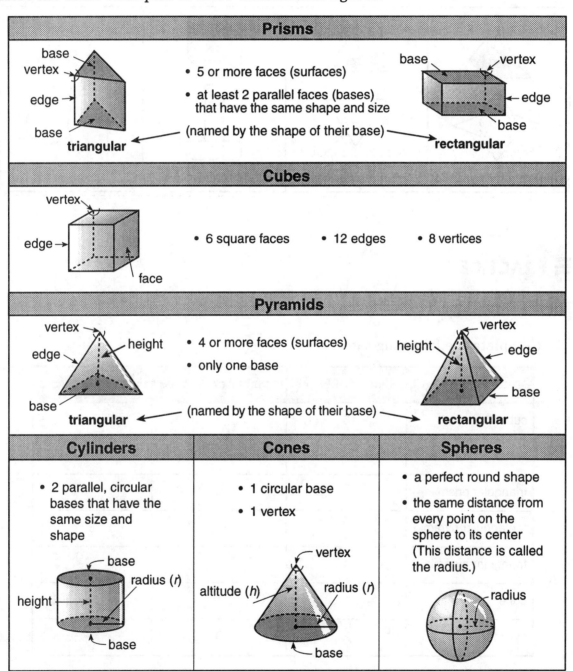

Prisms

base
vertex
edge
base
triangular

- 5 or more faces (surfaces)
- at least 2 parallel faces (bases) that have the same shape and size

(named by the shape of their base)

base   vertex
edge
base
rectangular

Cubes

vertex
edge
face

- 6 square faces   • 12 edges   • 8 vertices

Pyramids

vertex
edge
height
base
triangular

- 4 or more faces (surfaces)
- only one base

(named by the shape of their base)

vertex
height   edge
base
rectangular

Cylinders

- 2 parallel, circular bases that have the same size and shape

base
radius (*r*)
height
base

Cones

- 1 circular base
- 1 vertex

vertex
altitude (*h*)   radius (*r*)
base

Spheres

- a perfect round shape
- the same distance from every point on the sphere to its center (This distance is called the radius.)

radius

This is how the figures would look if they were laid flat on a surface.

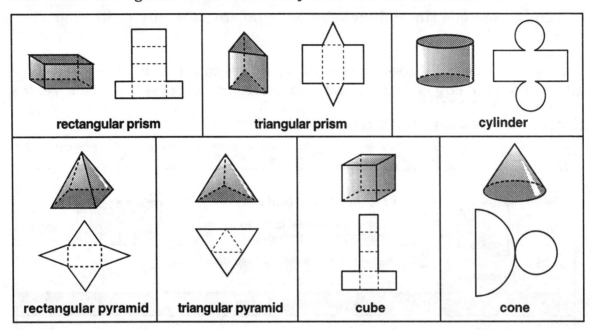

rectangular prism triangular prism cylinder

rectangular pyramid triangular pyramid cube cone

 **PRACTICE**

Directions: Complete the following problems.

1. Complete the following table.

Figure	Number of Faces	Number of Vertices	Number of Edges
cube	6		
rectangular prism			
triangular prism		6	
rectangular pyramid			8
triangular pyramid	4		
cone	1	1	
cylinder	2	0	

2. Describe the faces of a rectangular pyramid and a triangular pyramid.

   rectangular pyramid _____

   _____

   triangular pyramid _____

   _____

3. Describe the edges of a rectangular prism and a cube.

   _____

   _____

4. Circle the figure that does *not* belong in the group of figures pictured below.

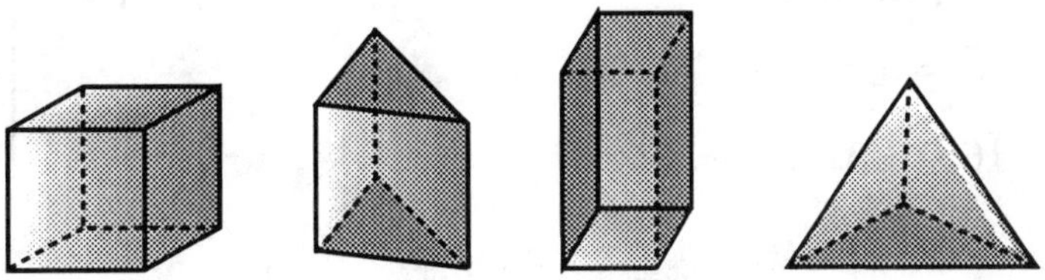

   Explain on the lines below why the figure you circled does *not* belong with this group.

   _____

   _____

   _____

Lesson 11: The Pythagorean Theorem

This lesson covers how to apply the Pythagorean principle to solve problems.

The **Pythagorean Theorem** states: *The square of the length of the hypotenuse (the side opposite the right angle) is equal to the sum of the squares of the lengths of the other two sides.*

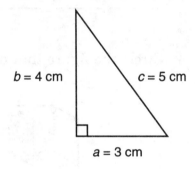

Here is how the theorem is stated in mathematical terms:

$$c^2 = a^2 + b^2$$

Basically, the theorem says that if you know the length of any two sides of a right triangle and know which side is the hypoteneuse, you can determine the length of the third side.

 **Example**

▶ If the theorem is correct, then 3^2 plus 4^2 should be equal to 5^2.

$$3^2 + 4^2 = 5^2$$
$$9 + 16 = 25$$
$$25 = 25$$

b = 4 cm   c = 5 cm

a = 3 cm

Example

▶ Find the length of the hypotenuse.

$$c^2 = a^2 + b^2$$
$$c^2 = 5^2 + 12^2$$
$$c^2 = 25 + 144$$
$$c^2 = \sqrt{169}$$
$$c = 13$$

The hypotenuse's length is 13 in.

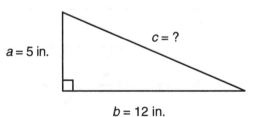

a = 5 in.

c = ?

b = 12 in.

☰ PRACTICE

Directions: Find the length of the third side for each triangle below. (Some of the squares will be perfect squares, that is, their square roots are whole numbers. Other squares are not perfect squares. Their square roots are difficult to determine without a calculator. Feel free to use a calculator whenever you need to.)

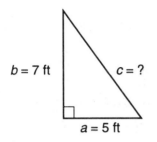

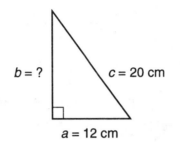

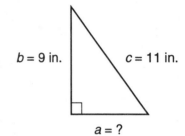

1. $c =$ _____

2. $b =$ _____

3. $a =$ _____

Special Right Triangles

Isosceles right triangle

45°–45°–right triangle (45°–45°–90°)

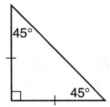

An isosceles right triangle has one 90° angle, two equal angles, and two equal sides.

$$\angle x + \angle x + 90° = 180° \qquad 45° + 45° + 90° = 180$$

$$2x + 90° = 180°$$

$$2x = 180° - 90°$$

$$x = \frac{90°}{2}$$

$$x = 45°$$

The ratio of the sides of an isosceles triangle is $x : x : x\sqrt{2}$

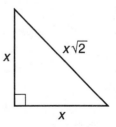

☰ Example

▶ One of the equal sides of a right isosceles triangle is 4. What is the measure of the hypotenuse (c)?

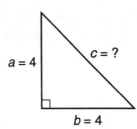

$$c^2 = a^2 + b^2 \qquad\qquad 4\sqrt{2} = c$$
$$c^2 = 4^2 + 4^2 \qquad \text{or use the ratio } x:\ x:\ x\sqrt{2}$$
$$c^2 = 16 + 16 \qquad\qquad 4:\ 4:\ 4\sqrt{2}$$
$$\sqrt{c^2} = \sqrt{32} \qquad\qquad c = 4\sqrt{2}$$
$$c = \sqrt{16}\sqrt{2}$$
$$c = 4\sqrt{2}$$

30°–60°–right triangle (30°–60°–90°)

A right triangle with two acute angles of 30° and 60°.

The ratio of the sides of a 30°–60°–90° right triangle is $x:\ x\sqrt{3}:\ 2x$

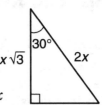

☰ Example

▶ The shortest side of a 30°–60°–90° right triangle is 5. What is the measure of the other sides?

$$a = x = 5$$
$$b = x\ \sqrt{3} = 5\sqrt{3}$$
$$c = 2x = 2(5) = 10$$

☰ PRACTICE

Directions: Complete the following problems:

1. If the hypotenuse in a right isosceles triangle is $9\sqrt{2}$, what is the measure of the two equal sides?

   _____

2. Complete the following table for a 30°–60°–right triangle.

Measure of hypotenuse	Measure of side opposite	
	30° angle	60° angle
12		
	9	
		$7\sqrt{3}$

Lesson 12: Congruency and Similarity

In math, when we say that figures are similar, we mean that their dimensions are proportional. (For a review of proportions, see Lesson 8.) This lesson covers how to use congruent and similar figures to solve problems.

Congruent Figures

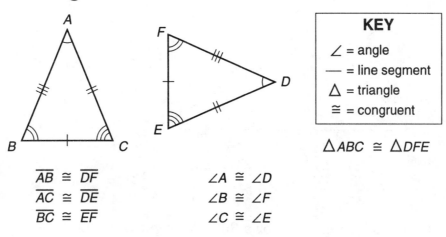

KEY

$\angle$ = angle

— = line segment

$\triangle$ = triangle

$\cong$ = congruent

$\triangle ABC \cong \triangle DFE$

$\overline{AB} \cong \overline{DF}$ $\angle A \cong \angle D$

$\overline{AC} \cong \overline{DE}$ $\angle B \cong \angle F$

$\overline{BC} \cong \overline{EF}$ $\angle C \cong \angle E$

Triangle *ABC* is congruent to triangle *DFE*.

☰ PRACTICE

Directions: Complete the following problems:

Figure *ABCDEF* is congruent to ($\cong$) *JKLMNO*

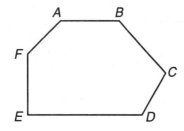
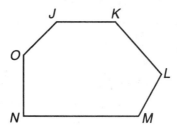

1. Which angle in *ABCDEF* is congruent with $\angle M$? ___$\angle D$___

2. $\overline{BC} \cong$ ___$\overline{KL}$ $\cong$___   3. $\overline{EF} \cong$ ___$\overline{ON}$ $\cong$___

4. Name two additional congruent sides. ___FA   OJ___

Similarity

Figures that have the same shape but not the same size are **similar figures**. The symbol for similar is ~.

 Example

▶ $\triangle FGH \sim \triangle LMN$

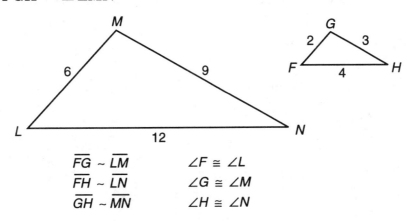

$$\overline{FG} \sim \overline{LM} \qquad \angle F \cong \angle L$$
$$\overline{FH} \sim \overline{LN} \qquad \angle G \cong \angle M$$
$$\overline{GH} \sim \overline{MN} \qquad \angle H \cong \angle N$$

 Similar figures are proportional.

 Example

▶ $\triangle ABC$ is similar to $\triangle DEF$. Find the length of side x.

Step 1: **Set up a proportion.**

$$\frac{8}{16} = \frac{12}{x}$$

Step 2: **Cross multiply.**

$$8 \times x = 16 \times 12$$
$$8x = 192$$

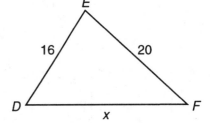

Step 3: **Divide.**

$$x = \frac{192}{8}$$

$$x = 24$$

 **Example**

▶ Two trees in a yard cast shadows one afternoon. The first tree, whose height is known to be 24 feet, cast a 32-foot shadow. The second tree cast a 40-foot shadow. What is its height?

The relationship between the trees' heights and their shadows is proportional—the sunlight is shining down at the same angle on both trees. Therefore, a proportion can be set up to describe the relationship.

Step 1: **Set up a proportion.**

$$\frac{\text{first tree's height}}{\text{first tree's shadow length}} = \frac{\text{second tree's height}}{\text{second tree's shadow length}}$$

$$\frac{24}{32} = \frac{n}{40}$$

Step 2: **Cross multiply.**

$$(24)(40) = 32n$$

$$960 = 32n$$

Step 3: **Divide.**

$$\frac{960}{32} = n \qquad \leftarrow \text{isolate the variable } n \text{ and do the division}$$

$$30 = n \qquad \leftarrow \text{second tree's height is 30 ft}$$

☰ PRACTICE

Directions: Complete the following problems.

1. In the grid below, draw a figure similar to figure *I*.

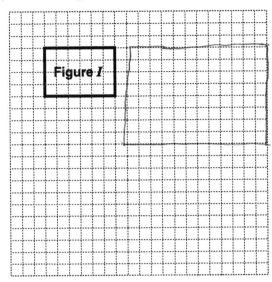

Figure *I*

2. △ *LMN* ~ △ *RST*

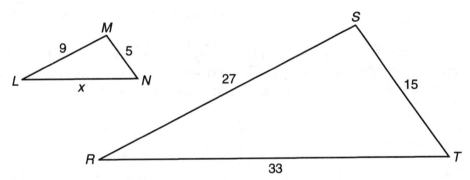

$x = \underline{\,11\,}$

3. $\bigcirc ABCDE \sim \bigcirc FGHIJ$

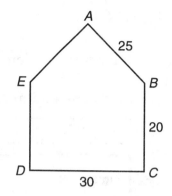

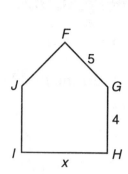

$x = \underline{6}$

4. Figure $RSTU \sim$ Figure $WXYZ$

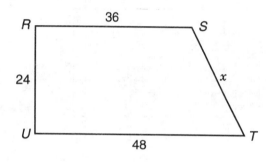

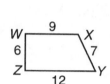

$x = \underline{28}$

5. Claire used a copy machine to make a copy of a 24 cm (width) by 28 cm (length) picture she had drawn. She reduced the size of the picture so that the length of the copy was 21 cm. What was its width?

$\underline{18 \text{ cm}}$

6. Tomas is making a scale model of the Washington Monument. The Monument's height is 169 m and each side at the base is 17 m wide. Frank decided to make his model 1.3 m tall. How wide should each side be at the base of his model?

_____

Lesson 13: Coordinate Geometry

This lesson explores geometric ideas using a coordinate plane.

The diagram below is called a **coordinate plane**. It has a **horizontal axis** called the **x-axis**, and a **vertical axis** called the **y-axis**. The point where the two axes intersect is called the **origin**.

The coordinate plane is divided in quadrants.

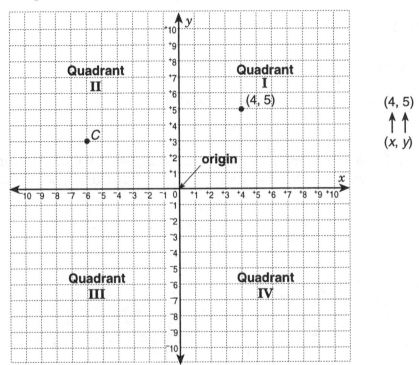

Points in the coordinate plane are described by **ordered pairs** (also known as **coordinates**). The *first* number (or the **abscissa**) describes its location on the **x-axis**. The *second* number (or the **ordinate**) in an ordered pair describes its location on the **y-axis**.

The ordered pair (4, 5), shown on the coordinate plane above, means that the point is located 4 units to the right of zero on the x-axis and 5 units above zero on the y-axis.

   What ordered pair describes point C? _____

On the x-axis, numbers to the right of zero are positive; numbers to the left of zero are negative.

On the y-axis, numbers above zero are positive; numbers below zero are negative.

(4, 5) is located in Quadrant I. Points in Quadrant I are (+, +)—except when they are at the origin.

Describe, in general terms, (x, y) in Quadrant IV.

_____

PRACTICE

Directions: Complete the following problems:

1. In which Quadrant are (x, y) both negative? _____

2. Graph the following coordinates: $(^-3, 2)$, $(4, 2)$, $(4, ^-2)$, $(^-3, ^-2)$. Connect the points in the order in which you graph them. Start and end at $(^-3, 2)$.

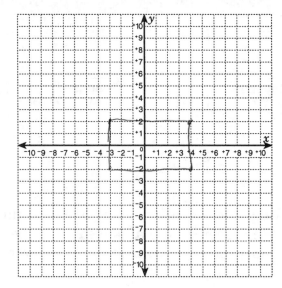

Describe the figure shown. _____

Directions: Use the following graph to answer questions 3 and 4.

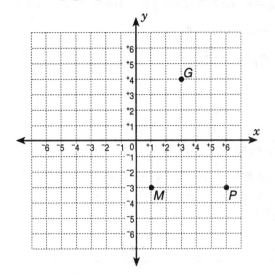

3. What are the coordinates of point M? $(^+1, ^-3)$ _____

4. What shape is made if you connect the points on the graph?

_____

5. The map below shows New York's counties.

   Use the map to complete the following.

   Part A: Locate (2, 3) and identify the county it lies in.

   _____ Chenango _____

   Part B: Give the coordinates of the county that you live in. __5,4__

   Part C: One of your friends calls you over the phone and tells you that his map does not show Fulton county. How can you help him locate Fulton county on his map?

   _____ 6,4 _____

   _____

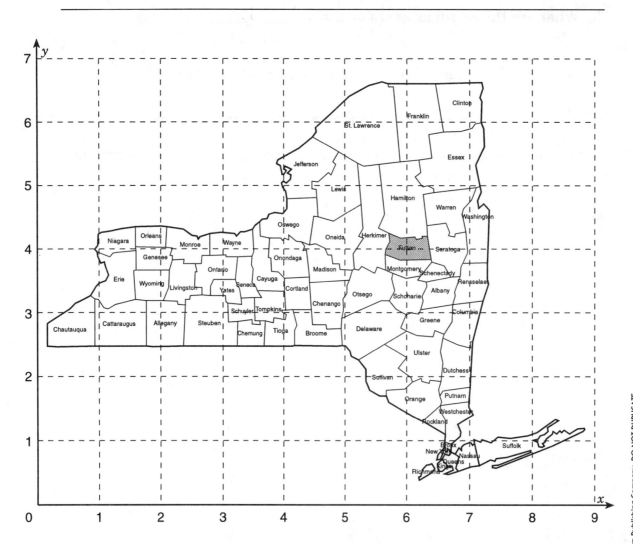

Lesson 14: Maps and Scale Drawings

This lesson shows you how to represent real objects or places using maps and scale drawings.

Scale

A **scale** is used in drawings to tell you what each unit represents in terms of the actual size of the object drawn.

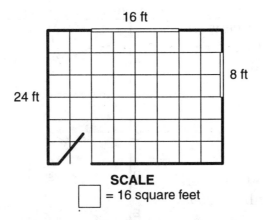

Scales are useful when you are drawing a model of an actual object or place. For example, if you decided to draw a model of a room in your house, you would want to create a scale to represent the actual size. In the drawing, each square unit represents sixteen square feet in actual size.

Scales are also used in maps to represent distance. For example, in the map below, $\frac{3}{4}$ inch is equal to 30 miles.

PRACTICE

Directions: Use the map to the right to answer questions 1–3.

1. The distance by road between Mosquito Flats and Buster is *about* how many miles?

   60 miles

2. The distance by road between Buster and Mooseville is *about* how many miles?

   45 miles

3. Which town is farther away by road from Mosquito Flats, Meadow Lark or Bass? *Estimate* how many miles farther.

   Bass , 15 miles

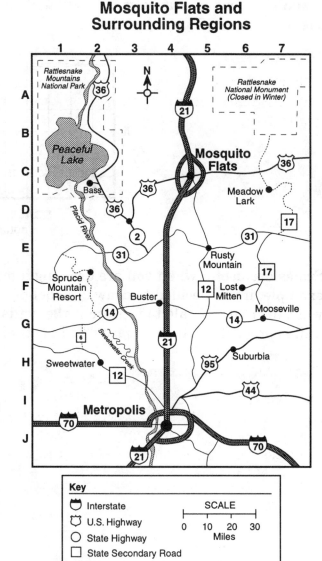

Mosquito Flats and Surrounding Regions

Key
- Interstate
- U.S. Highway
- State Highway
- State Secondary Road

SCALE
0 10 20 30
Miles

Lesson 15: Transformations

This lesson investigates both two- and three-dimensional transformations.

Transformations and Symmetry

Translations, reflections, and rotations are ways in which a figure can be transformed. Each one of these transformations also refers to a kind of symmetry.

Translation (slide)

When you move a figure without changing anything other than its position, it is called a **translation**, or a **slide**. Figures can be slid in any direction (up, down, right, left).

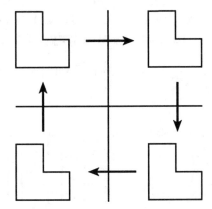

Translational symmetry

If you can slide a figure a certain distance in a given direction so that it lands on top of an identical figure, the two are said to have **translational symmetry**. Sometimes this can continue on in a pattern with any number of identical figures lined up at equal distances apart.

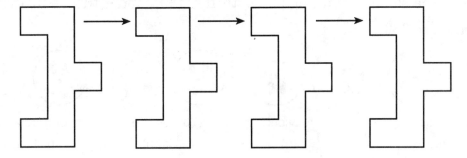

Reflection (flip)

When you flip a figure and create its mirror image, you have performed a **reflection**, or a **flip**. When a figure is reflected, there must be a line across which you flip it. This line is called a **line of reflection**, or a **line of symmetry**. When you are asked to identify or draw the reflection of a figure, this line must be given.

In the example to the right, triangle 2 is a reflection of triangle 1. The vertical line is the line of reflection or line of symmetry.

Reflectional symmetry

A figure has **reflectional symmetry** if there is a line of reflection through it, and its two halves are mirror images of each other. Sometimes a figure has reflectional symmetry in more than one direction. Reflectional symmetry is also known as **line symmetry**, **bilateral symmetry**, and **mirror symmetry**.

Letters are good examples of figures with reflectional symmetry. The dotted lines represent lines of symmetry.

Rotation (turn)

When you turn a figure around a certain point, a **rotation**, or **turning**, has been performed. A figure can be rotated in a number of different ways. A $\frac{1}{4}$ turn clockwise is the same as rotating 90°, $\frac{1}{2}$ turn = 180°, and $\frac{3}{4}$ turn = 270°. A full turn is equal to 360°.

| 90° rotation ($\frac{1}{4}$ turn) | 180° rotation ($\frac{1}{2}$ turn) | 270° rotation ($\frac{3}{4}$ turn) | 360° rotation (full turn) |

Rotational symmetry

If a figure can be rotated less than 360° around its point of rotation, so that it coincides with its original image, it is said to have **rotational symmetry**. The figure below has rotational symmetry.

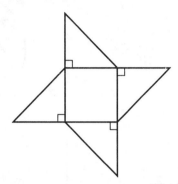

You can perform more than one kind of transformation on a figure. The figure below has been reflected across the *y*-axis and rotated 90°.

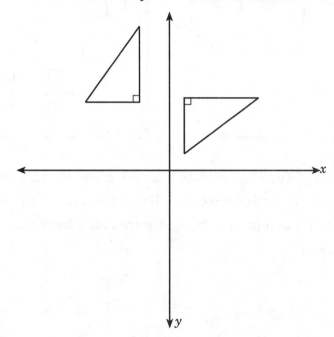

Asymmetry

Shapes that have no symmetry are called **asymmetric**. Each of the following figures is asymmetric.

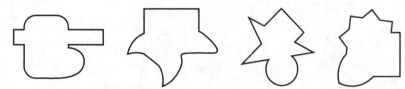

≡ PRACTICE

Directions: Identify which type or types of symmetry each figure or pattern has.

1.
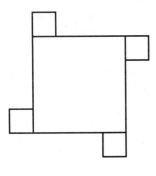

_____

3.

_____

2.
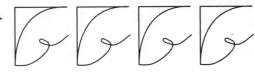

_____

4.
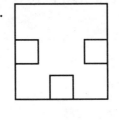

_____

Directions: For each figure below that has reflectional symmetry, draw the line or lines of symmetry. For each figure that has rotational symmetry, tell whether it has $\frac{1}{4}, \frac{1}{2}, \frac{3}{4}$ rotational symmetry. Some figures may have both reflectional and rotational symmetry.

5.

_____

7.
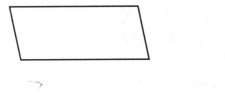

_____

6.

_____

8.

_____

© 1999 Buckle Down Publishing Company. DO NOT DUPLICATE.

Translations can also be applied to three dimensional figures. Look at the following shape.

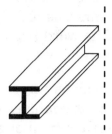

Example A is a reflection of the shape above, and Example B is a translation or slide of the original shape above.

A

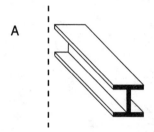

B

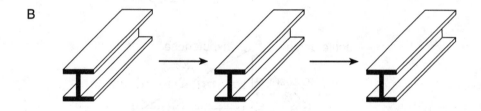

Lesson 16: Trigonometry Concepts

Many distances can be found by measuring directly with a ruler or tape measure. Some distances which cannot be measured directly can be found using the principles of **trigonometry**. The word trigonometry comes from some Greek words which mean "triangle measurement."

This lesson briefly explores and develops three of the special relationships that exist for all **right triangles**. All right triangles have a hypotenuse (the side opposite the right angle) and two other smaller sides (legs). Each acute angle is formed by what is refered to as an adjacent leg and the hypotenuse.

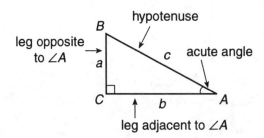

For acute $\angle A$, side b is the leg adjacent to $\angle A$ and side a is the leg opposite $\angle A$.

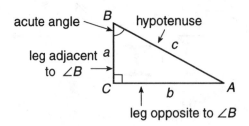

For acute $\angle B$, side a is the leg adjacent to $\angle B$ and side b is the leg opposite $\angle B$.

Tangent Ratio

The **tangent (tan)** ratio for an acute angle of a right triangle is the ratio of the length of the leg opposite the acute angle to the length of the leg adjacent to the acute angle. (For a review of ratio see Lesson 8)

$$\tan A = \frac{\text{length of opposite side}}{\text{length of adjacent side}} = \frac{a}{b}$$

≡ Examples

▶ Find the tan A in the right triangle shown.

$$\tan A = \frac{\text{length of opposite side}}{\text{length of adjacent side}} = \frac{5}{12}$$

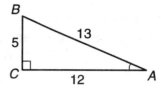

Find the tan B in the right triangle shown.

$$\tan B = \frac{\text{length of opposite side}}{\text{length of adjacent side}} = \underline{\hspace{2cm}}$$

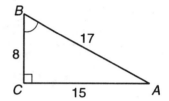

Sine Ratio

The **sine (sin)** ratio for an acute angle of a right triangle is the ratio of the length of the leg opposite the acute angle to the length of the hypotenuse.

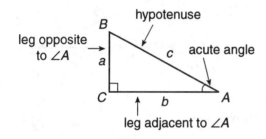

$$\sin A = \frac{\text{length of opposite side}}{\text{length of hypotenuse}} = \frac{a}{c}$$

≡ Examples

▶ Find the sin A in the right triangle shown.

$$\sin A = \frac{\text{length of opposite side}}{\text{length of hypotenuse}} = \frac{3}{5}$$

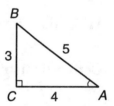

Find the sin B in the right triangle shown.

$$\sin B = \frac{\text{length of opposite side}}{\text{length of hypotenuse}} = \underline{\hspace{2cm}}$$

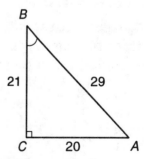

Cosine Ratio

The **cosine (cos)** ratio for an acute angle of a right triangle is the ratio of the length of the leg adjacent to the acute angle to the length of the hypotenuse.

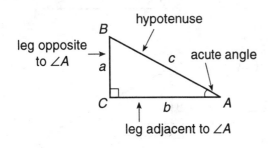

$$\cos A = \frac{\text{length of adjacent side}}{\text{length of hypotenuse}} = \frac{b}{c}$$

▤ Examples

▶ Find the cos A in the right triangle shown.

$$\cos A = \frac{\text{length of adjacent side}}{\text{length of hypotenuse}} = \frac{12}{13}$$

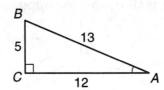

Find the cos B in the right triangle shown.

$$\cos B = \frac{\text{length of adjacent side}}{\text{length of hypotenuse}} = \underline{\hspace{2cm}}$$

What does cos B reduce to as a fraction? _____

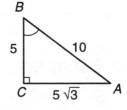

Convert this reduced fraction to a decimal. _____

You can also use a table to find the tangent, sine, and cosine of acute angles.

Trigonometric Table

Degrees	Sine	Cosine	Tangent
0	.0000	1.0000	.0000
5	.0872	.9962	.0875
10	.1736	.9848	.1763
15	.2588	.9659	.2679
20	.3420	.9397	.3640
25	.4226	.9063	.4663
30	.5000	.8660	.5774
35	.5736	.8192	.7002
40	.6428	.7660	.8391
45	.7071	.7071	1.0000
50	.7660	.6428	1.1918
55	.8192	.5736	1.4281
60	.8660	.5000	1.7321
65	.9063	.4226	2.1445
70	.9397	.3420	2.7475
75	.9659	.2588	3.7321
80	.9848	.1736	5.6713
85	.9962	.0872	11.4301
90	1.0000	.0000	....

(Leading zeros have been deleted.)

Example

If you know the measure of $\angle B = 60°$, you can find the cos B in the right triangle shown by using the table.

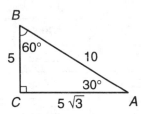

Go down to 60 in the Degrees column and then right to the Cosine column and write the number you find. ___.5___

The table gives a value for the cos 60° as 0.5000.

This is the same value you get when you calculate:

$$\cos B = \frac{\text{length of adjacent side}}{\text{length of hypotenuse}} = \frac{5}{10} = \frac{1}{2} = 0.5$$

 Example

Find the sin A in the right triangle shown by using the table.

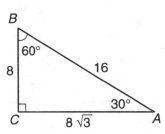

The measure of $\angle A = $ _____ °

The table gives a value for the sin 30° as __.5___.

This is the same value you get when you calculate:

$$\sin A = \frac{\text{length of opposite side}}{\text{length of hypotenuse}} = \frac{8}{16} = \frac{1}{2}$$

$$\frac{1}{2} = 0.5$$

Using the table or the sin ratio will give you the same answer.

SOHCAHTOA

≡ PRACTICE

Directions: In exercises 1 and 2, find the tan A.

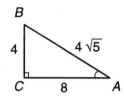

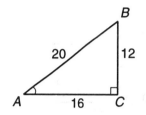

1. tan A = $\frac{4}{8} = \frac{1}{2}$

2. tan A = $\frac{12}{16} = \frac{3}{4}$

Directions: In exercises 3 and 4, find the sin B.

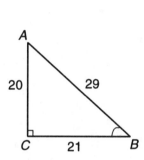

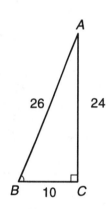

3. sin B = $\frac{20}{29}$

4. sin B = $\frac{24}{26} = \frac{12}{13}$

Directions: In exercises 5 and 6, find the cos A.

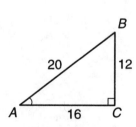

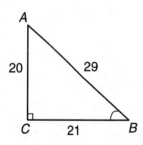

5. cos A = $\frac{16}{20} = \frac{4}{5}$

6. cos A = $\frac{20}{29}$

Directions: Use the Trigonometric Table on page 91 to answer problems 7–10.

7. sin 45° = ___.7071___

8. tan 45° = ___1.0___

9. cos 85° = ___.0872___

10. tan 15° = ___.2679___

Put Your Skills to the Test

1. Look at the diagram below. Line *a* is parallel to line *b*, and line *c* is a transversal.

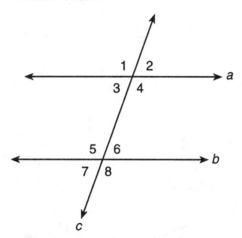

Which two angles are supplementary?
A. ∠1 and ∠4
B. ∠2 and ∠6
C. ∠5 and ∠6
D. ∠6 and ∠7

2. Right triangle *ABC* is similar to right triangle *DEF*.

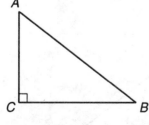

Which of the following is a true statement?
A. ∠*A* is congruent to ∠*B*
B. ∠*B* is congruent to ∠*E*
C. $\overline{AC}$ is congruent to $\overline{FE}$
D. $\overline{AB}$ is congruent to $\overline{DE}$

3. Two lines that intersect to form a right angle are called —
A. parallel.
B. perpendicular.
C. transversal.
D. acute.

4. Which of the figures below is *not* a polygon?

A.

B.

C.

D.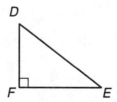

Directions: Use the coordinate plane below to answer questions 5 and 6.

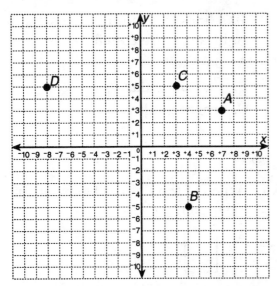

5. What are the coordinates of point *A*?

   A. (⁻7, 3)

   B. (4, ⁻5)

   C. (7, 3)

   D. (7, ⁻3)

6. If you connect the following points *ABDCA* in the order given, which of the following polygons would be formed?

   A. triangle

   B. quadrilateral

   C. pentagon

   D. octagon

7. If the figure below was translated, how would it look?

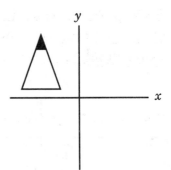

A.

C.

B.

D.

8. Floods washed out the road that ran south from Wrangle to Hoopersville, so Tony had to drive the long way from Wrangle to Hoopersville by way of Red Rock. How many miles farther was the detour route he took from Wrangle to Hoopersville than the regular route?

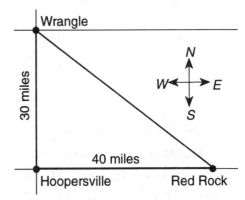

   A. 50 miles   C. 60 miles

   B. 55 miles   D. 65 miles

9. Which of the following is *not* a property of a rectangle?

   A. a quadrilateral

   B. a quadrilateral with only one pair of parallel sides

   C. a parallelogram with 4 right angles

   D. opposite sides are equal and parallel

10. Triangle *ABC* is a right triangle.

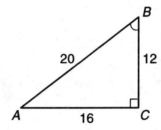

   What are the numerical values of the sine and tangent of angle *B*?

   sine *B*_____   tangent *B*_____

11. The figure below is right triangle *ABC*, and $\angle A = 55°$ and is not congruent to $\angle C$. Calculate the measure in degrees of $\angle C$.

Show your work.

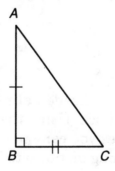

Answer: _____

Explain in words the relationship between $\angle A$ and $\angle C$ that allows you to calculate the measure of $\angle C$.

_____

_____

Directions: Use the map below to answer problem 12.

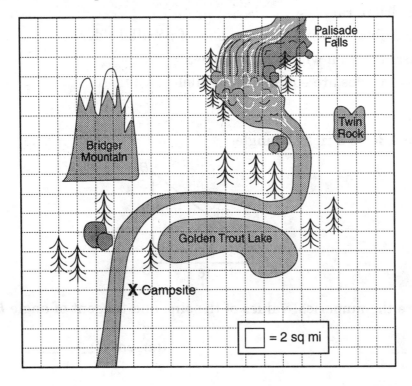

12. You have discovered that your map of the Palisade Falls trail is incorrect.

Part A

Correct the map by redrawing Bridger Mountain so that it is translated two units to the left.

Part B

You decide to bike along the Palisade Falls trail from your campsite at Golden Trout Lake to Twin Rock. Using the scale from your map, approximate how many miles you can bike on the trail before you have to get off and walk the remaining distance to Twin Rock.

Show your path on the map above.

Answer: _____

Explain how you determined your answer.

_____

_____

unit 4

Measurement

Lesson 17: Units, Tools, Precision, and Reasonableness

This unit focuses on choosing the right units and tools to solve problems involving measurements in real-world situations.

Measurement Systems

You can measure using customary or metric units of measurement.

Metric units are related through the use of prefixes.

Prefixes and Their Meaning

kilo	hecto	deka	deci	centi	milli
thousands	hundreds	tens	ten**ths**	hundred**ths**	thousand**ths**

The tables below show the most common units of measurement in metric and customary units.

Length

Metric	Conversion
*milli*meter (mm) thin like a wire	1 mm $\frac{1}{10}$ cm
*centi*meter (cm) width of your little fingernail	1 cm = 10 mm
meter (m) a little bit taller than a kitchen table	1 m = 100 cm
*kilo*meter (km) about 6 city blocks	1 km = 1,000 m

U.S. Customary	Conversion
inch (in.) about the diameter of a quarter	1 in. $\frac{1}{12}$ ft
foot (ft) the length of a ruler	1 ft = 12 in.
yard (yd) the length of a yardstick	1 yd = 3 ft 1 yd = 36 in.
mile (mi) approximately 10 city blocks	1 mile = 5,280 ft

Mass/Weight

Mass and weight are essentially the same in everyday life. However, mass is not really the same as weight. **Mass** refers to the quantity of an object. **Weight** refers to the force of gravity exerted on the object. On the moon, for example, your mass would be the same as it is on the earth, but you would weigh only one-sixth as much.

Metric	Conversion
milligram (mg) about the weight of the wing of a housefly	1 mg $\frac{1}{1000}$ g
gram (g) about the weight of a paper clip	1 g = 1,000 mg
kilogram (kg) about the weight of one volume of an encyclopedia	1 kg = 1,000 g

U.S. Customary	Conversion
ounce (oz) about the weight of a slice of bread	1 oz $\frac{1}{16}$ lb
pound (lb) about the weight of a hammer	1 lb = 16 oz
ton (T) about the weight of a small car	1 T = 2,000 lb

Capacity

Metric	Conversion
milliliter (mL) about what an eyedropper holds	1 mL $\frac{1}{1000}$ L
liter (L) a large plastic soda bottle contains two liters	1 L = 1,000 mL
kiloliter (kL) about the size of a large wading pool	1 kL = 1,000 L

U.S. Customary	Conversion
tablespoon (tbs)	1 tbs = 3 tsp
cup (c)	1 c = 16 tbs 1 c = 8 fluid oz
pint (pt)	1 pt = 2 c
quart (qt)	1 qt = 2 pt 1 qt = 4 c
gallon (gal)	1 gal = 4 qt 1 gal = 8 pt 1 gal = 16 c

Conversions

In metric as well as in customary units, when you are converting *within the same system* . . .

- from a smaller unit to a larger unit you **divide**.

  For example: 24 in. (smaller unit) to ft (larger unit)

$$24 \div 12 = 2 \text{ ft}$$

- from a larger unit to a smaller unit you **multiply**.

  For example: 3 m (larger unit) to cm (smaller unit)

$$3 \times 100 = 300 \text{ cm}$$

PRACTICE

Directions: Complete the following conversions for problems 1–4.

1. 5 gal = _____ pt

2. 48 oz = _____ lb

3. 16 km = _____ m

4. 5.75 kg = _____ g

5. Which unit of measure would you use to measure the following? Complete the table.

Description	Metric	Customary
glass of milk		ounce
an apple		
your weight		
length of a wall		

6. Victor has a load of three boxes for his truck. The boxes weigh 1,242 lb, 559 lb, and 1,109 lb. What is the total weight of the boxes in tons and pounds?

   _____ T _____ lb

7. Mushava's car holds 60 liters of gasoline in the gas tank. He used up most of a tankful of gas on a trip. It took 59.32 liters to fill up the tank again. How many milliliters of gas had been left over from the first tankful?

   _____

8. Jim bought 2 quarts of soda pop to share with some friends. How many 10-ounce glasses can he completely fill with 2 quarts of soda pop?

   _____

   How much soda will be left over?

   _____

9. Angelica wants to walk 20 km. She plans to stop and rest every 5,000 meters. Including the stop she will make at the end of the walk, how many times will she stop?

   _____

Temperature

System	Unit	Water freezes at . . .	Water boils at . . .
Metric	Celsius – °C	0°C	100°C
Customary	Fahrenheit – °F	32°F	212°F

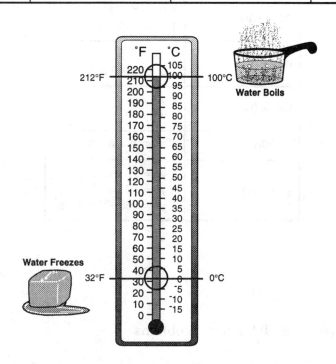

Water Boils

Water Freezes

PRACTICE

Directions: Complete the following problems.

1. Which would be the best temperature for swimming outside: 10°C or 32°C?

   _____

2. The temperature was 35°F. By midnight, it had dropped 42°F. What was the temperature by midnight?

   _____

Time

The basic unit of time, the second (s), is the same in both systems.

Unit	Conversion
minutes (min)	1 min = 60 s
hour (hr)	1 hr = 60 min 1 hr = 3,600 s
day (d)	1 d = 24 hr 1 d = 1,440 min
week (wk)	1 wk = 7 d 1 wk = 168 hr
month (mo)	1 month = 4 wk
year (yr)	1 yr = 12 month 1 yr = 52 wk 1 yr = 365–366 days

PRACTICE

Directions: Complete the following problems.

1. You leave home at 12:25 P.M. and arrive at the mall at 1:19 P.M. How long did it take you to get to the mall?

   _____

2. At what time do you leave home for school in the morning? _____

   At what time do you arrive at school? _____

   What is the elapsed time? _____

Selecting Appropriate Units and Tools

When you are faced with an unfamiliar measurement situation, there are several things to think about before you make your measurement.

As you evaluate the measurement situation, you need to decide on:

the appropriate **unit**
and
the appropriate **tool**.

Choosing a unit

Ask yourself these three questions:

1. **What kind of measurement** is this: length, weight, time, area, capacity, etc.?

2. Will you make the measurement in the **standard or metric system**?

3. **Which unit** do you need within that measuring system?

☰ Example

▶ A farmer is hauling oranges to sell. He knows he must stay within the weight limits set by the state transportation department for that particular section of the highway. How can he be sure he does not overload his truck?

Step 1: What kind of measurement?

weight

Step 2: Standard or metric?

After inquiring, he learns that the state measures weight in standard units.

Step 3: Which unit of weight in the standard system is needed?

Crates and trucks are measured in either pounds or tons.

Next, you must decide on the appropriate tool or tools for measuring.

Choosing a measuring tool

Ask yourself these two questions:

1. **Which tool** is best for the particular measurement situation?

2. **What degree of accuracy** does the situation call for?

☰ Example

▶ . . . Back to the farmer and his oranges.

Step 1: **Which tool** is best for the particular measurement situation?

Since the farmer is weighing something, he needs a scale. It's probably not practical to assume that he has a scale large enough to weigh the loaded truck. However, he most likely has a scale large enough to weigh one crate. He should weigh one crate with his scale. His measurement needs to be in pounds.

Next, the farmer should multiply the weight of one crate by the number of crates that he plans to put on the truck.

Finally, he should add in the weight of the truck itself. (The truck manual will give him this measurement.)

Step 2: **How accurate** should he be?

On the one hand, he would like to make each trip pay by loading to the maximum. On the other hand, an overloaded truck will result in a hefty fine. The best plan would be to choose one of the fullest crates to weigh. When he multiplies its weight by the total number of crates, his weight estimate will be a little high, but he isn't likely to get a fine.

Accuracy and Precision

No matter what you are measuring, or what instrument you are using, you can never really get an exact measurement. The best you can hope for is a close approximation.

Accuracy in measurement refers to how close your value is to the actual measurement and how carefully a measurement instrument is used.

Precision in measurement refers to how sure you are that you can repeat the measure and get the same measurement. Precision depends on the units used; the smaller the unit, the more precise the measurement.

☰ Example

▶ Let's see how precisely we can measure this black line.

Look at Ruler A. The black line is about $1\frac{1}{2}$ (or 1.5) inches long.

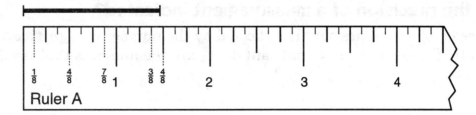

Ruler A

Even though the edge of the black line is not exactly on the $\frac{4}{8}$ (or $\frac{1}{2}$) mark, you know that it is between $\frac{3}{8}$ and $\frac{4}{8}$.

Now look at Ruler B. With this ruler, the line measures about $1\frac{7}{16}$ (or 1.4375) inches long. You can get a more precise measure of the length of the line because the ruler is marked in sixteenths.

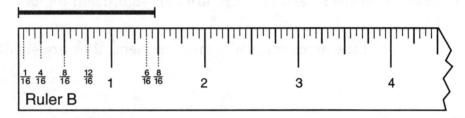

Ruler B

Could you get a measure that is even more precise?

Look at Ruler C.

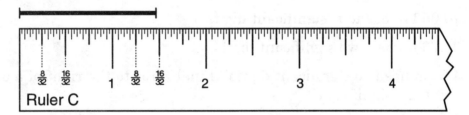

Ruler C

With Ruler C, you can get a closer estimate of the length of the black line. It is about $1\frac{15}{32}$ (or 1.46875) inches long.

How do you show precision?

If you are using fractions, *do not reduce the fraction* to lowest terms. The denominator of the fraction tells the smallest fraction of a unit on the measuring instrument. $1\frac{15}{32}$ in. is more precise than $1\frac{1}{2}$ in.

What is the precision of a measuring instrument?

The precision of a measuring instrument is the *smallest* fractional or decimal division on the instrument.

How is the precision of a measurement indicated?

The precision of a measurement is indicated by the number of **significant digits** in that measurement. Significant digits are the numbers that result from measurement.

 Example

▶ How many significant digits are in 0.007400 m?

In a decimal fraction (when the number is between 0 and 1), the zeros immediately following a decimal point are *not* significant.

Since 0.007400 m is a decimal fraction, the first three zeros are *not* significant digits. However, the last two zeros are part of the preciseness of the measure. There are four significant digits.

When zeros are part of the preciseness of a measurement, they are significant digits.

Examples

▶ 3.021 grams has four significant digits. (The 0 here is part of the preciseness of the measurement.)

70.05 km has four significant digits.

0.076 in. has two significant digits.

4.0 cm has two significant digits. (Final zeros to the right of a decimal point are significant.)

9000.0 mg has five significant digits.

The pen below measures *about* 13 cm or 132 mm.

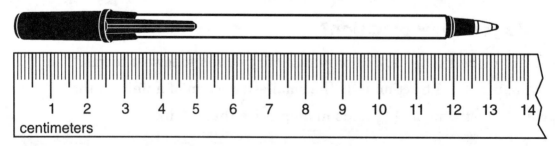

If you measure the pen to the nearest centimeter, it measures 13 cm. This measure has two significant digits, 1 and 3.

If you want to convert the measure from centimeters to millimeters, the pen measures approximately 130 mm. How many significant digits does this measure have? Two, zero is not a significant digit because the measurement is still precise to the nearest cm, or to the nearest 10 mm.

However, if you use 132 mm as the measure of the pen, the measurement has three significant digits: 1, 3, and 2. Even if you write the measure as 13.2 cm, the number of significant digits is still three.

Which is more precise: 13 cm or 132 mm? _____

When solving problems involving measurement, make sure you think about:

- **The measurement** – Are you measuring length, volume (capacity), weight, or some other quantity?

- **The units** – Are you measuring in metric or customary units? Within those systems, what units are you using (for example, inches, feet, or yards)? Do you need to make any conversions?

- **The instrument (or tool)** – What is the best instrument to use to find the measurement you are looking for? For example, would you want to use a 12-inch ruler to find the length of a door? Yes. What about using a ruler to find the length of a football field? Probably not.

- **Reasonableness of your answer** – Is your answer reasonable? If someone says that a three-story building measures "about 40," is it 40 inches, 40 feet, 40 yards, or 40 miles tall? The reasonable answer is 40 feet.

- **Precision** – How precise do you need to be? If you are measuring a chemical solution, for example, you have to be more precise than if you are measuring a cup of sugar.

When you are making calculations with more than one measurement, your answer is only as precise as the *least precise* measurement. To round to the proper number of significant digits, round to the measurement with the **least number of significant digits**.

Example

▶ 120.7 lb + 112 lb = 232.7

The least number of significant digits is 3. The sum should have 3 significant digits. Round 232.7 to 233.

PRACTICE

Directions: Complete the following problems.

1. Arthur is training to run a race in the famous Liberty Relay Meet next spring. He will be running the 100 m dash. He wants to measure his progress between now and then.

   What kind of measurement(s) should be used: length, weight, time, area, or capacity?

   _____

   Which unit(s) does he need within the measuring systems?

   _____

   Which tool(s) would be *best* to use?

   _____

   How accurate and/or precise does he need to be? Explain.

   _____

   _____

2. Which of the following situations should be *most* concerned with having precise measurements? Explain why.

   _____ a truck driver planning how far to drive in a day

   _____ a bricklayer planning to build a garden wall

   _____ a scientist mixing chemicals for an experiment

   _____

   _____

3. Two pieces of copper pipe were welded together. The pipes were 41 cm and 20.8 cm. What was the total length of the welded pipe? _____

   What is the least number of significant digits? _____

   Round the pipe length to the proper number of significant digits. _____

Lesson 18: Formulas

This lesson focuses on developing your skill to apply formulas in measurement problems.

Using Formulas to Solve Measurement Problems

A **formula** is a general rule that is written using letters and symbols. For example:

$$S = 180°(n - 2) \qquad P = 2(l) + 2(w) \qquad A = b \times h \qquad V = Bh \qquad d = rt$$

Distance formula

The formula $d = rt$ shows the relationship between **distance** (d), **rate** (r), and **time** (t). If two of the values are known, the third value can be found by using the same methods used for solving equations.

 Example

On their way to the state meet, the track team traveled in a school bus for 2 hours at 55 miles per hour. How far did the team travel?

$$d = rt \qquad r = 55 \, mph \qquad t = 2 \, hours$$

Step 1: **Substitute the known values.**

$$d = 55 \times 2$$

Step 2: **Solve the equation.**

$$d = 110$$

Here is a simple way to remember how to use the formula for distance, rate, and time:

- To find distance: Cover the letter d. You are left with rate multiplied by time.

$$d = r \times t$$

- To find rate: Cover the letter r. You are left with distance divided by time.

$$r = d \div t$$

- To find time: Cover the letter t. You are left with distance divided by rate.

$$t = d \div r$$

Rate

A **rate** is a ratio used to compare two different units. For example, miles per hour, miles per gallon, dollars per hour, meters per second, kilometers per hour, etc.

Some ways of expressing rate are:

mi/hr, mph, or miles/hour km/hr mi/gal hr/m

Example

▶ Julie drove 63 miles in one hour. What is the rate in mi/min?

$$\frac{\text{mi}}{\text{hr}} \rightarrow \frac{63}{60} \quad (1 \text{ hour} = 60 \text{ minutes})$$

$$\frac{63}{60} = 1.05 \text{ mi/min}$$

Another way to find rate

Example

▶ James drove 126 km in 2 hours. At this rate, how many hours would it take to drive 315 km?

Step 1: **Set up a proportion.**

$$\frac{\text{km}}{\text{hr}} \rightarrow \frac{126}{2} = \frac{315}{n}$$

Step 2: **Multiply to get the cross products.**

$$126 \times n = 2 \times 315$$
$$126 \times n = 630$$

Step 3: **Simplify the equation so that n stands alone.**

$$\frac{\cancel{126} \times n}{\cancel{126}} = \frac{630}{126}$$
$$n = 5$$

At the rate of 126 km/2 hr, it will take 5 hours to drive 315 km.

Step 4: **Check your answer.**

Replace n with your answer.

$$126 \times n = 2 \times 315$$
$$126 \times 5 = 2 \times 315$$
$$630 = 630$$

 **PRACTICE**

Directions: Complete the following problems.

1. A car travels at 65 miles per hour for 4 hours. What is the distance traveled?

   _____

2. Harriet's grandparents live 256 miles away. Because of road construction, it took Harriet and her parents 5 hours to drive there. What was the mi/hr rate of travel?

   _____

3. Jayne is a bicycle racer. She enters a citizens' race and travels 30 miles in 1.5 hours. What is her rate of speed?

   _____

4. Angelic paid $5.10 for 6 hours of parking. What is the hourly rate?

   _____

5. Pablo read 45 pages in one hour. What is his reading rate in pages per minute?

   _____

Other Formulas

Sum of the inside angles of a polygon

The general rule to find the sum of the interior angles of a polygon is:

$$S = 180°(n - 2)$$

where n = number of sides

$(n - 2)$ = number of triangles formed by diagonals

Every diagonal line has to be drawn from the same vertex.

$$S = 180°(n - 2)$$
$$S = 180°(6 - 2)$$
$$S = 180°(4)$$
$$S = 720°$$

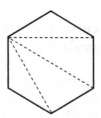

The diagonal lines divide this hexagon into 4 triangles. The sum of all the angles inside a triangle is 180°. This tells you that if you add the four triangles (180° + 180° + 180° + 180°) or multiply 180° × 4, the answer will be equal to 720°.

☰ PRACTICE

Directions: Complete the table below. Draw the triangles inside each figure.

Number of sides	Polygon	Sum of measure of vertex angles
4	☐	360°
_____	▭	_____
5	⬠	_____
6	⬡	720°
_____	⬡	_____

Perimeter

Perimeter is the distance around a polygon.

To find the perimeter of a polygon, add the
length of all the sides (*s*).

$$P = s + s + s \ldots$$

$$P = 2 + 6 + 3 + 7$$

$$P = 18 \text{ cm}$$

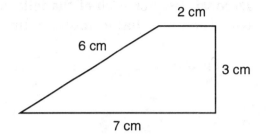

The following table tells you what formula to use to find the perimeter of
different polygons.

Figure	Formula	Example
any polygon 4 ft 3 ft 2 ft 5 ft 7 ft	$P = s + s + s \ldots$	$P = 3 + 4 + 2 + 7 + 5$ $P = 21$ ft
regular polygon (all sides and all angles are equal) 4.5 in.	$P = $ number of sides x l	$P = 6$ x 4.5 $P = 27$ in.
rectangle 5 m w 3 m l	$P = 2(l) + 2(w)$ or $P = 2(l + w)$	$P = 2(5) + 2(3)$ $P = 10 + 6$ $P = 16$ m $P = 2(5 + 3)$ $P = 2(8)$ $P = 16$ m

☰ PRACTICE

Directions: For each of the following questions, write the formula that you will use. Then use that formula to find the perimeter of the figure.

1. Formula: _____ $P =$ _____

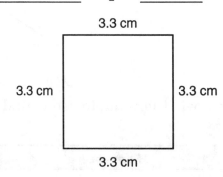

3.3 cm

3.3 cm   3.3 cm

3.3 cm

2. Formula: _____ $P =$ _____

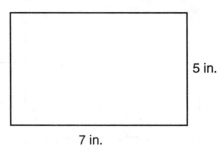

5 in.

7 in.

Circumference

Here is a simple way to remember the formula for **circumference**.

Circumference $(C) = \pi \times$ diameter (d)

☰ Example

▶   The circumference of a 12 oz. soda can is 21 cm. Find its diameter to the nearest tenth.

Cover the letter d and you are left with C divided by π.

$d = C \div \pi$

Step 1: Substitute the known values.

$\pi = 3.14$ $C = 21$ cm

$21 \text{ cm} = (3.14)d$

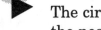

116

Step 2: Solve the equation.

$$\frac{21.0}{3.14} = \frac{\cancel{3.14}d}{\cancel{3.14}}$$

$$6.7 \text{ cm} = d$$

You can also use the formula: $C = 2\pi r$

 **PRACTICE**

Directions: Complete the following problems:

1. What is the circumference of a circle with a radius of 20 cm? _____

2. What is the diameter of a circle with a circumference of 18 m? _____
   Round to the nearest whole number.

3. What is the circumference of this jumbo party pizza? _____

$r = 1.5$ ft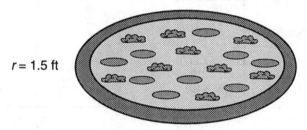

Area

Area is the measure of the region inside a closed plane figure. Area is measured in square units. The table below shows formulas to find the area of different geometric shapes.

Name			Example
square	side (s), side (s)	$A = s^2$	$s = 3$ in. $A = (3 \text{ in.}) \times (3 \text{ in.})$ $A = 9 \text{ in.}^2$
rectangle	width (w), length (l)	$A = lw$	$l = 10$ cm; $w = 5$ cm $A = 10 \text{ cm} \times 5 \text{ cm}$ $A = 50 \text{ cm}^2$
triangle	height (h), base (b)	$A = \frac{1}{2}bh$ or $A = \frac{bh}{2}$	$b = 4$ m; $h = 3$ m $A = \frac{4 \text{ m} \times 3 \text{ m}}{2}$ $A = \frac{12}{2}$ $A = 6 \text{ m}^2$
parallelogram	height (h), base (b)	$A = bh$	$b = 8.5$ yd; $h = 14$ yd $A = 8.5 \text{ yd} \times 14 \text{ yd}$ $A = 119 \text{ yd}^2$
trapezoid	base₁ (b_1), height (h), base₂ (b_2)	$A = \frac{1}{2}h(b_1 + b_2)$ or $A = \frac{h(b_1 + b_2)}{2}$	$b_1 = 3$ ft; $b_2 = 5$ ft; $h = 4$ ft $A = \frac{4 \text{ ft}(3 \text{ ft} + 5 \text{ ft})}{2}$ $A = \frac{4 \text{ ft}(8 \text{ ft})}{2}$ $A = \frac{32}{2} = 16 \text{ ft}^2$
circle	radius (r), diameter (d)	$A = \pi r^2$	$r = 6$ cm; $\pi \approx 3.14$ $A = 3.14 \times (6)^2$ $A = 3.14 \times 36 \text{ cm}^2$ $A = 113.04 \text{ cm}^2$

≡ PRACTICE

Directions: Find the area.

1. What is the area of a wall that measures 5 meters by 4 meters? _____

2. What is the area inside this tractor tire? _____

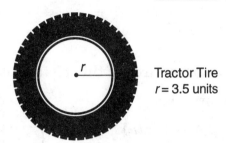

Tractor Tire
$r = 3.5$ units

3. What is the area of a triangle with a base of 4.6 cm and a height of 3.9 cm?

_____

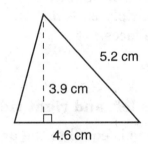

5.2 cm
3.9 cm
4.6 cm

4. What is the approximated area of the shaded arrow? _____

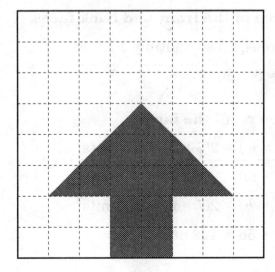

Surface Area

Surface area is the measure of the outside of a three-dimensional object. It is measured in square units.

Surface area of rectangular solids

This is how the faces of a **rectangular prism** would look if they were laid flat on a surface.

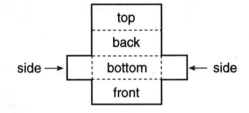

 Example

▶ What is the total surface area of this rectangular prism?

You can use this formula:

$$SA = 2(lw) + 2(hw) + 2(lh)$$

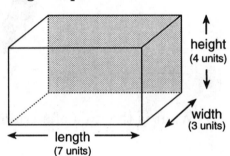

Step 1: Find the area of the top and the bottom faces.

The area of the top face ($l \times w$) is equal to the area of the bottom face ($l \times w$). Therefore, multiply $2(l \times w)$ to find the area of the faces.

$2(7 \times 3) = 42$ units^2

Step 2: Find the area of the left and right sides.

The area of the left side is equal to the area of the right side, so multiply $2(h \times w)$.

$2(4 \times 3) = 24$ units^2

Step 3: Find the area of the front and back faces.

Both faces are equal so multiply $2(l \times h)$.

$2(7 \times 4) = 56$ units^2

Step 4: Add the area of all the faces.

$$2(l \times w) = 2(7 \times 3) = 42 \text{ units}^2$$

$$2(h \times w) = 2(4 \times 3) = 24 \text{ units}^2$$

$$2(l \times h) = 2(7 \times 4) = 56 \text{ units}^2$$

$$42 + 24 + 56 = 122 \text{ units}^2$$

Surface area of a cylinder

The surface area of a **cylinder** is the area of the two circular bases added to the area of the side.

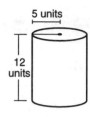

This is how the faces of the cylinder would look if they were laid flat on a surface.

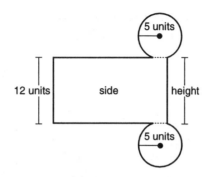

≡ Example

▶ What is the total surface area of the cylinder shown above? You can use the formula: $SA = 2\pi rh + 2\pi r^2$

Step 1: **Find the area of the lateral side.** Multiply the circumference ($2\pi r$) by the height (h). (Use 3.14 for π)

$2\pi rh$

$2(3.14 \times 5 \times 12) = ?$

$2(188.4) = 376.8 \text{ units}^2$

Step 2: **Find the area of the circular bases.** The formula to find the area of one circular base is $A = \pi r^2$.

Since there are 2 circular bases, multiply the area by 2.

$2\pi r^2$

$2(3.14 \times 5^2) = ?$

$2(3.14 \times 25) = ?$

$2(78.5) = 157 \text{ units}^2$

Step 3: **Add the area of the lateral side and the two bases.**

$SA = 2\pi rh + 2\pi r^2$

$SA = 376.8 + 157$

$SA = 533.8 \text{ units}^2$

≡ PRACTICE

Directions: Find the total surface area of the following figures.

1. What is the total surface area of the rectangular solid? _____

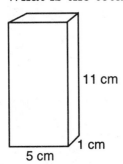

11 cm

1 cm

5 cm

2. What is the total surface area of the cylinder?_____

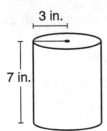

3 in.

7 in.

3. What is the surface area for an open piece of pipe that has a radius of 4 cm and a length of 9 cm?

_____

Volume

Volume is the amount of space in a three-dimensional figure. Volume is measured in cubic units (for example: cm^3, in.^{3}, ft^3, m^3, etc.).

Volume of prisms

To find the volume (V) of a **prism**, multiply the area of the base (B) by the height (h).

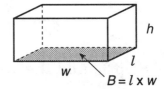

h

l

w

$B = l \times w$

$$V = Bh$$

The area of the base (B) of a rectangular prism = length (l) × width (w).

$$V = l \times w \times h$$

© 1999 Buckle Down Publishing Company. DO NOT DUPLICATE.

☰ Example

▶ What is the volume of this rectangular prism?

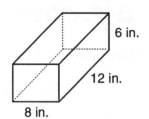

6 in.

12 in.

8 in.

$V = 12 \times 8 \times 6$

$V = 576$ in.^{3}

Volume of cylinders

To find the volume (V) of a cylinder, multiply the area of the base ($B = \pi r^2$) by the height (h).

$$V = Bh \qquad \text{or} \qquad V = \pi r^2 h$$

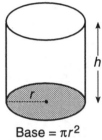

h

r

Base $= \pi r^2$

☰ Example

▶ What is the volume of this glass?

$r = 2$ in.
$h = 7$ in.

$V = \pi r^2 h$

$V = 3.14 \times 2^2 \times 7$

$V = 3.14 \times 4 \times 7$

$V = 87.92$ in.^{3}

88 in.^{3} (Rounded to the nearest whole number.)

≡ PRACTICE

Directions: Find the volume of the following figures.

1. What is the volume of the following figure? _____

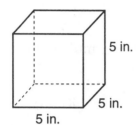

5 in.

5 in.

5 in.

2. What is the volume of a rectangular solid that has a length of 2 meters, a width of 3 meters, and a height of 2 meters?

_____

3. What is the volume of the cylinder below? _____

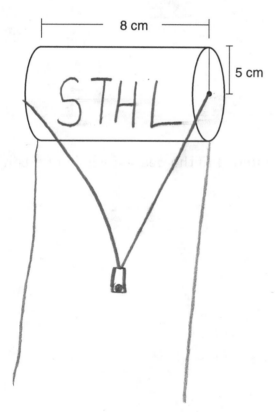

8 cm

5 cm

STHL

Lesson 19: Data Analysis and Statistics

This lesson will explore how to display, describe, and compare data.

Statistics

Statistics is a set of methods used to collect, organize, describe, and analyze numerical data.

The numbers below are the minutes walked by a group of junior high students in a walk-a-thon.

45, 60, 75, 55, 40, 90, 20, 40, 50, 60, 40

This set of data by itself does not give you much information if you want to summarize, describe, or make decisions based on it.

In order to make use of the data, you need to organize it. One way of organizing data is with measures of central tendency. **Measures of central tendency** use one number to represent all the numbers in the set.

The **mode**, **median**, and **mean** can all be used to describe the central tendency of the data.

One way to remember them is:

MODE = most often

MEDIAN = middle

MEAN = average

Mode

The **mode** is the number that appears most often in a set of numbers. The "mode" is whatever is most used, repeated, etc.

 **Example**

▶ Ms. Johnson, the physical education teacher, wants to know what time occurred most often.

45, 60, 75, 55, 40, 90, 20, 40, 50, 60, 40

In other words, Ms. Johnson wants to know the mode.

Solution: Find the number that appears most often.

When looking for the mode, it is usually helpful to **arrange the numbers in order.**

20, **40, 40, 40**, 45, 50, 55, 60, 60, 75, 90

40 appears 3 times

We can say that, for this group of students, the mode is 40.

 In a set of numbers, there might be one mode, **more than one** mode, or no mode at all.

Median

The **median** is the middle number in a group of numbers **arranged in order of value.**

 Example

Mr. Alvarez, the science teacher, **wants to select the student who was in the middle of the group of walkers. What information about the times should he look for?**

45, 60, 75, 55, 40, 90, 20, 40, 50, 60, 40

Mr. Alvarez should look for the median.

Solution: To find the median, arrange the numbers in order, **then find the middle number.**

20, 40, 40, 40, 45, 50, 55, 60, 60, 75, 90

This set has 11 numbers. Find the middle number.

20, 40, 40, 40, 45, |**50,**| 55, 60, 60, 75, 90

five numbers before—**50**—five numbers after

The number 50 divides the set into two equal parts.

If the median is between two numbers, add the two **numbers and divide** by 2.

Example

What is the median of the following set of scores?

29, 31, 33, 35, 37, 39, 41, 41

The median of this set of scores is between 35 and 37.

Add: $35 + 37 = 72$

Divide by 2: $\frac{72}{2} = 36$

The median of this set of scores is 36.

Mean

The **mean** (also commonly called "the average") is the sum of the numbers in a group divided by how many numbers are in that group. It is affected by all the numbers in the set.

Example

Mrs. Parker, the math teacher, wants to know the average number of minutes the students walked.

45, 60, 75, 55, 40, 90, 20, 40, 50, 60, 40

Solution: To find the mean, set up this equation:

$$\text{mean} = \frac{\text{sum of the numbers}}{\text{how many numbers}}$$

$$\text{mean} = \frac{575}{11} = 52.27 \ldots$$

$$\text{mean} = 52 \text{ (rounded to the nearest whole number)}$$

Use of the Measures of Central Tendency

How do you decide whether you want to use the mean, median, or mode? That depends on what information you are looking for.

Example

Monica is setting sales goals for the art club fund-raiser. The club is selling posters and mugs to raise money for a trip to a museum. The list below shows the amounts raised by 13 members of the club during the last fund-raiser.

$10 $15 $20 $20 $20 $20 $25 $25 $30 $40 $46 $90 $120

Mode = 20   Median = 25   Mean = 37

If Monica were to set goals based on this data, what measure of central tendency should she use?

If she wants to set goals based on what *most* members actually raised during the last fund-raiser, she should use the mode. The amount reported most often was $20.

If Monica wants to set goals based on the total amount raised during the last fund-raiser, she should use the mean, which was $37.

And if she wants to set goals based on the midpoint of her data, she should use the median, which was $25.

Monica could use any of these measures in presenting goals to her group. Which one she chooses will depend on what she wants to accomplish. She might choose the mode or median if she wants to be realistic about what members might actually be expected to sell. If she wants to encourage members to do more than might reasonably be expected (based on past sales), she might choose the mean. (The mean is not very accurate in describing a set of data that has extreme numbers, as in this example, where the extremes are $10 and $120.)

 PRACTICE

Directions: Complete the following problems.

1. A community theater group has 20 members. Most of the members are 16 years old. What statistical measure does this statement represent?

   _____

Directions: Use the following table to answer questions 2–4.

2. What is the mean of the test scores?

   _____

3. What is the median of the test scores?

   _____

4. What is the mode of the test scores?

   _____

Test	Scores
Exam 1	92
Exam 2	95
Exam 3	90
Exam 4	89
Exam 5	79
Exam 6	88
Exam 7	90

Range

Range is one measure of the **variability** of the data. (Variability tells how the numbers vary or change.) To find the range, find the difference between the largest and smallest number in the set of data.

≡ Example

▶ Mr. Lewis, the art teacher, wants to draw a graph of the walk-a-thon. To draw the scale, he needs to know the difference between the shortest and longest time that the students were walking.

Walking times: 45, 60, 75, 55, 40, 90, 20, 40, 50, 60, 40

Find the range. (This is another situation in which it might help to arrange the numbers in order.)

20, 40, 40, 40, 45, 50, 55, 60, 60, 75, **90**

The largest number is 90, the smallest is 20.

Find the difference.

90 − 20 = 70

The range is 70.

≡ PRACTICE

Directions: Use the table below to complete question 1.

Test	Scores
Exam 1	92
Exam 2	95
Exam 3	90
Exam 4	89
Exam 5	79
Exam 6	88
Exam 7	90

1. What is the range of the test scores?

_____

Data Analysis

Graphic representations of data—such as tables, charts, and graphs—help you to do a variety of things, including:

- summarize information
- show trends
- make predictions
- draw conclusions

Tables and charts

Tables and charts are used to present information in a way that is easy to read and understand.

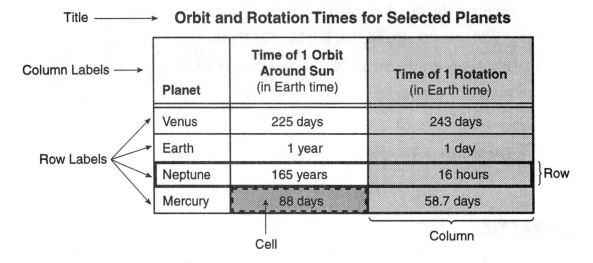

Orbit and Rotation Times for Selected Planets

When reading a chart or table, follow these steps:

Step 1: **Read the title.** It will help you understand what the chart or table is about.

Step 2: Find out what information is recorded in the **rows** and **columns**. On the top row of a table, you will usually find **labels** that tell what information is in the columns. Each box of information is called a **cell**. A cell can be identified by the name of its column and row.

Step 3: Locate the information you need by following the appropriate column and row to the correct cell. For example, if you wanted to know how long it takes Neptune to rotate once, you would look in row 3 (Neptune), column 2 (Time of 1 Rotation), and find that it takes 16 hours.

Frequency tables

When you have a lot of data in a set, one way to organize it is to use a **frequency distribution table**. It tells you at a glance not only what numbers are in the data set, but how many of each number are included.

≡ Example

▶ Here are a list of test scores from a group of 8th grade students: 85, 85, 90, 90, 95, 100, 95, 100, 85, 90, 85, 100, 85, 90, 95, 100, 90, 85, 85, 90, 85, 95

It's hard to do anything with this data set unless it is organized. A frequency table can put it all into something easy to read and understand.

Score	Frequency
85	8
90	6
95	4
100	4

To find the mean score of the students in this table, first, you must find the total number of points scored by the class. To do this, multiply each score by its frequency:

$$85 \times 8 \qquad 90 \times 6 \qquad 95 \times 4 \qquad 100 \times 4$$

Then find the sum of those products:

$$680 + 540 + 380 + 400$$

The final step is to divide the total number of points by the total number of students in the class (which is the sum of the frequencies).

$$\text{mean} = \frac{\text{sum of student scores}}{\text{number of students}}$$

$$\text{mean} = \frac{2000}{8 + 6 + 4 + 4}$$

$$\text{mean} = \frac{2000}{22} = 90.\overline{90} \quad (\overline{n} \text{ is another way of showing that the number repeats infinitely.})$$

The mean score was 90.9.

☰ PRACTICE

Directions: Use the table below to complete the following problem.

Time Spent Watching TV	Frequency of Response
1 hour	15
2 hours	22
3 hours	29
4 hours	17

1. A math class surveyed students at school to find out how much time they typically spend each day watching TV. The frequency table above gives the results of the survey:

   To the nearest tenth of a hour, how much time does the average student spend watching TV per day?

   _____

Graphs

Pictographs, bar graphs, line graphs, and circle graphs are commonly used types of graphs.

Pictographs use pictures or symbols to compare data.

Computers Available at the Public Library

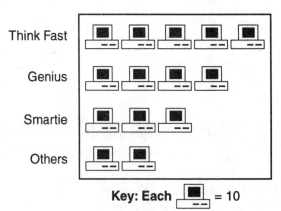

Key: Each 🖥 = 10

Bar graphs are generally used to compare amounts. A bar graph can show a reader how quantities compare without requiring the reader to do any computations.

Bar graphs can use vertical bars (as in the example) or horizontal bars.

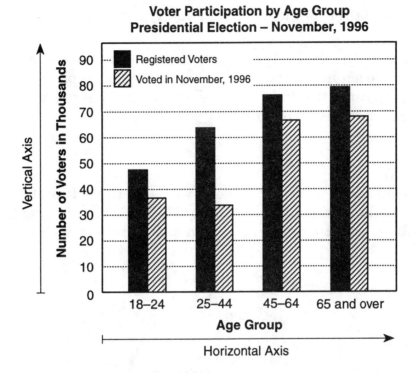

Line graphs are usually best for showing trends or changes over a period of time. They show increases and/or decreases in data. Line graphs are made by plotting points on a graph to represent data and then connecting those points.

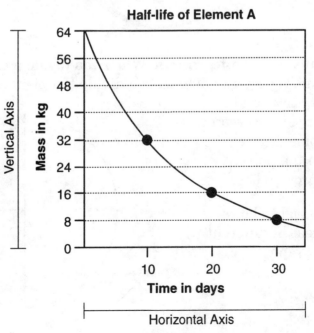

When reading a bar or line graph, follow these steps.

Step 1: Read the **title** of the graph. Make sure you understand what kind of information is being presented.

Step 2: Read the **labels** of the horizontal and vertical axes.

Step 3: Determine the **scale**. The scale is the number of units represented between each line marked along an axis of the graph. For example, in the line graph, the scale for the vertical axis (mass in kilograms) is marked in intervals of 8 units.

Circle graphs are used to show parts of a whole. Each part can be expressed as a percentage. The sum of all the parts equals 100%. A circle graph shows information at one particular time. It does not show trends or changes over a period of time.

Types of Materials Recycled

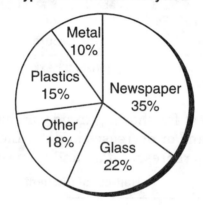

Circle graphs are often called **pie charts**. When you divide a circle into two equal parts, each part represents 50%. If you divide the pie into 4 equal parts, each part represents 25%, and so on. This means that you can read a circle graph with some degree of accuracy even when the percent information is not provided.

The example on the right shows the approximate areas of different percents in a circle graph.

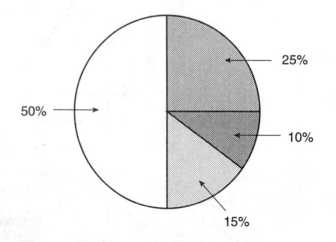

Evaluating Representations of Data

The same data can be represented in different ways. Some formats are more appropriate than others for certain kinds of data. The table below tells which format is usually best for which type of data.

Format	Type of Data
line graph	trends over time
bar graph	comparing amounts
circle graph	parts of a whole
table or chart	organizing numbers or things

 PRACTICE

Directions: Use the information below to create two different kinds of graphs. You may use all or part of the information. Remember to title your graphs and label all their parts.

End-of-School Party Activities

	Karaoke/ Singing	Games	Movies	Dancing
Time	Number of Students Participating			
7:00 P.M.	32	17	15	36
8:00 P.M.	24	33	20	23
9:00 P.M.	26	31	10	33
10:00 P.M.	18	19	55	8

☰ Put Your Skills to the Test

1. What is the total surface area of a rectangular solid with a width of 3 feet, a length of 5 feet, and a height of 7 feet?

   A.   15 ft^2

   B.   71 ft^2

   C. 105 ft^2

   D. 142 ft^2

2. The high temperatures for one summer week in the town of Mulberry are shown in the table below.

Day	Temperature
Sunday	98°F
Monday	95°F
Tuesday	97°F
Wednesday	90°F
Thursday	91°F
Friday	91°F
Saturday	89°F

   What was the mean temperature during this week?

   A. 89°F

   B. 91°F

   C. 93°F

   D. 98°F

3. A group of students was asked to name their favorite after-school activity. The chart below shows the results of the survey.

   Favorite After-school Activity

Sports & Games	60%
Reading	17%
Eating	8%
Sleeping	10%
Watching TV	5%

   How would the information look in a circle graph?

   A.

   B.

   C.

   D.

4. For the middle school dance, the social club wants to hang a banner all the way around the lunchroom. The two longer sides of the lunch room measure 50 feet each. The width of the lunchroom is 30 feet. The social club will use donated rolls of butcher paper that are each 60 feet long. How many rolls of butcher paper should the social club ask for to have enough paper to go all the way around the room one time?

A. 1 roll
B. 2 rolls
C. 3 rolls
D. 4 rolls

5. You want to show how sales of a new computer have risen and fallen over the last 12 months. Which format or formats listed below is most appropriate to show the data?

A. bar graph
B. circle graph
C. line graph
D. table or chart

6. If adult tickets to the rodeo are $5.95 and children's tickets are $3.89, which is the *best estimate* of how much it would cost a family of two adults and three children to attend the rodeo?

A. $19
B. $21
C. $22
D. $24

7. James is conducting an experiment in which he varies the amount of both sunlight and water for some barley plants. The plants are watered once a week. Plant A gets 8 oz. of water, Plant B gets 125% of the water that Plant A gets, Plant C gets twice the water that Plant A gets, and Plant D gets $\frac{3}{4}$ the water that Plant C gets. All four plants are in the group that gets 8 hours of sunlight a day. How much water is needed to water these four plants each week?

A. 26 oz
B. $37\frac{1}{4}$ oz
C. 40 oz
D. 46 oz

8. At New York City Bank's grand opening, there is a 2-liter bottle filled with dimes. If you have a 50-milliliter cup filled with dimes at home, how can you *best estimate* the number of dimes in the 2-liter bottle?
(Hint: 2 liters = 2,000 milliliters)

Show your work or explain in words how you determined your answer.

Estimate Answer:

_____

_____

9. Jenna is drawing a map of a remote wildlife preserve in the Yukon territory for a Canadian map company. She will be using the metric system. Explain what kind of measurement(s) she will use (length, weight, time, area, capacity) and which unit(s) she needs within the measuring system. Make sure you include in your explanation how accurate and/or precise she needs to be.

Answer: _____

_____

_____

_____

_____

10. A group of six organizations made the following donations to charity last year:

$30,000	$32,000	$33,000
$35,000	$36,500	$62,000

They used the mean value of the group's donations as a standard for requesting contributions from other organizations.

Part A

What is the mean and range of the donations?

Show your work.

Mean: _____   Range: _____

Part B

What measure of central tendency should this group use to request contributions from other organizations?

Answer: _____

138

Unit 5

Uncertainty

Lesson 20: Probability

Lesson 20: Probability

Probability is a measure of the likelihood that an event will occur. Another word for probability is **chance**.

In mathematics, probability is expressed as a number between 0 and 1 (including 0 and 1). What does this mean?

A **probability of 0** means that the event *will not* happen. For example, what is the likelihood that root beer will pour from the sky the next time it rains? The probability is zero. This is an event that will never happen.

A **probability of 1** means that the event *will* happen. For example, what is the likelihood that the sun will shine in the Sahara Desert this year? The probability is one. This is an event that will definitely happen.

≣ Example

▶ The weather forecaster says that the probability of rain tomorrow is 75%. This means that out of 100 days with the same weather conditions, it would be likely to rain on 75 of those days.

The forecast also means that there is a 25% chance that it will *not* rain tomorrow.

Which has a greater chance of happening tomorrow: having a rainy day or not having a rainy day?

Since 75% is greater than 25%, the probability of having rain is greater than that of not having rain.

Probability can be expressed in different ways.

Percent: 75%

Decimal: 0.75

Ratio: 75:100 or $\frac{75}{100} = \frac{3}{4}$ (in lowest terms)

Chances: 75 in 100

Experimental Probability

Experimental probability is the probability of an event based on an actual experiment.

≡ Example

▶ The table below shows the outcomes from an experiment in which two coins were tossed ten times.

Tosses	1	2	3	4	5	6	7	8	9	10
Outcomes	HT	HH	TT	TH	HT	TH	TH	HT	HT	TH

H = head   T = tail

To find experimental probability of an event [Exp P (E)], use this formula:

$$\text{Exp } P \text{ (E)} = \frac{\text{number of actual outcomes of the event}}{\text{number of trials in the experiment}}$$

Based on the experiment, what is the probability of HT?

[In mathematical language: What is Exp P (HT)?]

Step 1: Find the number of actual outcomes of the event.

In the coin toss experiment, there are 4 HT events.

Step 2: Find the number of trials in the experiment.

There are 10 trials in the experiment.

Step 3: Plug in the information in the formula.

$$\text{Exp } P \text{ (E)} = \frac{\text{number of actual outcomes of the event}}{\text{number of trials in the experiment}}$$

$$\text{Exp } P \text{ (HT) } \frac{4}{10} = \frac{2}{5} \text{ (in lowest terms)}$$

PRACTICE

Directions: Use the information in the table on the previous page to answer the following questions.

1. Find the Exp P (HH). _____

2. Find the Exp P (TT). _____

3. Find the Exp P (TH). _____

Counting Procedures

In probability experiments, one of the simplest ways of determining the possible outcomes of the experiment is to use a counting procedure.

Tree diagrams

A **tree diagram** is an easy counting procedure that can be used in probability experiments.

▤ Example

► The spinner below is spun twice. What are the chances of it landing once on black and once on white?

Spinner Results		
1st Spin	**2nd Spin**	**Possible Combinations**
B	B	B B
	W	B W
W	B	W B
	W	W W

The tree diagram shows that if the first spin landed on black (B), the second spin could land on either black (B) or white (W). The possible combinations when the first spin is B are 2 blacks (BB) or black and white (BW).

The tree diagram also shows that if the first spin landed on white, the second spin could also land on either black or white. The possible combinations when the first spin is W are white and black (WB) or 2 whites (WW).

So there are a total of four possible combinations when a spinner is spun twice: BB, BW, WB, and WW. Of those four possible outcomes, there are two that show the spinner landing once on black and once on white: BW and WB.

PRACTICE

Directions: What if the spinner in the previous example was spun 3 times? In the space below, make a tree diagram showing all the possible combinations of spins.

First Spin   Second Spin   Third Spin   Combinations

Directions: Use the tree diagram you created to answer questions 1–3.

1. How many total possible outcomes are there? _____

2. How many combinations of 1 black and 2 whites are possible? _____

3. List the combinations of 1 black and 2 whites.

_____

_____

Multiplication

You can also determine the total possible outcomes of an event by using multiplication.

▶ Example

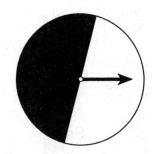

Imagine that you spin the spinner at the right 4 times. How many total possible outcomes are there?

You could draw a tree diagram, but multiplication is faster.

There are 4 spins.

Each spin has 2 possible outcomes, either black or white.

The number of total possible outcomes is $2 \times 2 \times 2 \times 2 = 16$.

▦ PRACTICE

Directions: Use the spinner above to complete questions 1–3.

1. What are the total possible outcomes in 6 spins of the black and white spinner?

   _____

2. Imagine a spinner with 3 colors: black, white, and blue. What are the total possible outcomes if you spin it 4 times?

   _____

3. If you have 2 number cubes, each one numbered 1 through 6 on the six faces, and you toss them one time, how many possible outcomes are there?

   _____

© 1999 Buckle Down Publishing Company. DO NOT DUPLICATE.

Theoretical Probability

You use **theoretical probability** when you cannot base your observation on an actual experiment. In other words, based on some observations, you will **infer**, **predict**, or **guess** what will happen.

The difference between experimental probability and theoretical probability is that with experimental probability you actually record all the outcomes. The more you increase the number of tries related to an experimental probability, the closer the outcomes will be to the theoretical probability.

Determining odds

What are the odds (chances) for an event to happen or not to happen?

 **Example**

> Imagine that you have entered your name 5 times in a drawing for a free-all day pass to rides at Ocean City Amusement Park. If there are 100 entries in the drawing, what are your odds of winning the pass?
>
> You have 5 in 100 chances of winning, or 5%.

What is the chance that you will *not* win the free pass? A 5% chance of winning also means that you have a 95% chance of not winning the free pass.

Probability of simple events

Simple events are events in which all possible outcomes are equally likely to happen. To find the probability of simple events follow these steps.

Step 1: **Find the number of successful outcomes.**

Step 2: **Find the total number of possible outcomes.**

Step 3: **Use the formula.**

$$P = \frac{\text{number of successful outcomes}}{\text{number of total outcomes}}$$

Express the fraction in lowest terms.

Example

A cube numbered 1 through 6 is rolled. What is the probability that the number 3 will show on the top side?

Step 1: **Find the number of successful outcomes.**

How many number 3s are on the cube?

The number of successful outcomes = 1

Step 2: **Find the total number of possible outcomes.**

How many numbers could possibly appear?

The number of possible outcomes = 6

Step 3: **Use the formula.**

$$P = \frac{\text{number of successful outcomes}}{\text{number of total outcomes}}$$

$$P = \frac{1}{6}$$

The probability of the number 3 showing on the top of the cube is 1 in 6.

This probability can also be expressed as:

0.166 . . .

16.6% (or 17%—rounded to the nearest whole number)

What is the probability of the number 7 showing on the top side of the cube?

There are no 7s on the cube. This event will not occur. The probability of this event happening is 0.

What is the probability of a number 1 through 6 showing on the top side of the cube?

$$P = \frac{6}{6} = 1$$

The probability of this event happening = 1.

≡ PRACTICE

Directions: Use the following information to answer questions 1–3.

José sent 6 entries for a chance to win a trip to the Everglades. There were a total of 5,000 entries sent.

1. What is the probability that José will win the trip? _____

2. What are the odds *against* winning the trip? _____

   Express it as a percent.

3. Which has a greater chance of happening—winning or *not* winning?

   _____

4. Ariana has a box of six donuts. Three of the donuts have strawberry filling. One has cream filling, and two have lemon filling. What are the chances that Ariana will choose a lemon-filled donut?

   _____

   What are the odds that she will *not* choose a strawberry-filled donut?

   _____

   Of all her choices, which event has the *least* chance of happening? Explain or show how you got your answer.

   _____

   _____

   _____

Probability of Independent Events

What you have done so far is to find the probability of simple events—one event occurring one time. What if you want to find the probability of two or more events occurring *at the same time but independent of each other*?

≡ Example

▶ Dylan has 6 neckties: one red, one blue, two striped, and two plaid. He has 4 dress shirts: one white, one blue, and two gray. If Dylan reaches into his closet without looking, what is the probability that he will pick a plaid tie *and* a gray dress shirt?

Step 1: **Find the probability of the first event. (P_1)**

picking a plaid tie

$$P_1 = \frac{2}{6} = \frac{\text{number of plaid ties}}{\text{total number of ties}} = \frac{1}{3}$$

Step 2: **Find the probability of the second event. (P_2)**

picking a gray dress shirt

$$P_2 = \frac{2}{4} = \frac{\text{number of gray shirts}}{\text{total number of shirts}} = \frac{1}{2}$$

Step 3: **Multiply. $P = P_1 \times P_2$**

$$P = \frac{1}{3} \times \frac{1}{2}$$

$P = \frac{1}{6}$ Probability of picking a plaid tie and a gray dress shirt.

≡ PRACTICE

Directions: Use the information in the previous example to answer questions 1–5.

1. What is the probability of picking a striped tie and a gray shirt?

   _____

2. What is the probability of picking a red tie and a white shirt?

   _____

3. What is the probability of picking a blue tie and a gray shirt? _____

4. Which of the above events (from problems 1, 2, or 3) is the *most* likely (has the highest probability) to occur?

   _____

5. Which of the events (from problems 1, 2, or 3) is the *least* likely to occur?

   _____

Probability of Dependent Events

To find the probability of dependent events (when results of one event affects the result of the other events) follow these steps.

 **Example**

> ▶ There are 7 marbles in a bowl; 3 are black and 4 are red. Two were picked at random one after the other. What is the probability of choosing a black marble first and a red marble second?

Step 1: **Find the probability of the first event.**

$$P_1 = \frac{\text{number of successful outcomes}}{\text{number of possible outcomes}}$$

$$P_1 = \frac{3}{7}$$

Step 2: **Find the probability of the second event.**

$$P_2 = \frac{\text{number of successful outcomes}}{(\text{number of possible outcomes}) - 1}$$

There are only 6 marbles left in the bowl. (The first marble was not returned to the bowl. $7 - 1 = 6$)

$$P_2 = \frac{4}{6} = \frac{2}{3} \leftarrow \text{(expressed in lowest terms)}$$

Step 3: **Multiply $P_1 \times P_2$.**

$$\frac{3}{7} \times \frac{2}{3} = \frac{6}{21} = \frac{2}{7} \leftarrow \text{(expressed in lowest terms)}$$

▤ PRACTICE

Directions: Use the information below to answer the questions.

Forrest has a box of 36 chocolate candies, all of which look alike. Nine of the candies have walnut chips in them. Six of the candies are chocolate-covered cherries.

1. What is the probability that the first chocolate candy taken from the box will contain walnut chips?

   _____

2. If the first chocolate taken from the box is a walnut chip, what is the probability that the second candy chosen will be a chocolate-covered cherry?

   _____

Probability of Mutually Exclusive Events

To find the probability of mutually exclusive events (events that cannot both happen at the same time: *either A or B*), you find the sum of the probabilities.

▤ Example

▶ There are 15 marbles in a bag: 1 orange, 3 black, 5 green, and 6 yellow. What is the probability of choosing a black or a yellow marble?

Step 1: **Find out the number of each successful outcome.**

   3 black marbles

   6 yellow marbles

Step 2: **Find out the total number of possible outcomes.**

   15 marbles

Step 3: **Write each probability as a fraction.**

   $\frac{3}{15} = P$ of black marbles

   $\frac{6}{15} = P$ of yellow marbles

Step 4: **Add.** Express the answer in lowest terms.

$$\frac{3}{15} + \frac{6}{15} = \frac{9}{15}$$

$$\frac{9}{15} = \frac{3}{5}$$

The probability of choosing a black or a yellow marble is $\frac{3}{5}$.

 **PRACTICE**

Directions: Use the information in the previous example to answer the question.

1. What is the probability of choosing an orange or green marble?

_____

Probability Based on a Sample

To find the probability of an event based on a sample follow these steps.

 **Example**

▶ Before selecting the classroom colors, a random survey of 10 students was conducted to determine color preferences. The table shows the results.

Colors	Preferences
Red	3
Green	5
Blue	2

Based on the results shown in the table, if 30 students are going to vote, how many students would choose red?

Step 1: **Find the probability of the event using the information from the sample.**

$$P = \frac{\text{number of students who prefer red}}{\text{total number of students in sample}} = \frac{3}{10}$$

Step 2: **Write a proportion.**

$$\frac{\text{number of students who prefer red}}{\text{total number of students in sample}} = \frac{\text{all students who prefer red}}{\text{total number of students voting}}$$

$$\frac{3}{10} = \frac{x}{30}$$

Step 3: **Solve the proportion.**

$$\frac{3}{10} = \frac{x}{30}$$

$$10x = 90$$

$$\frac{10x}{10} = \frac{90}{10}$$

$$x = 9$$

Of the 30 students in the classroom, 9 students will **probably choose red.**

≡ PRACTICE

Directions: Complete the following problem.

1. Lights For Ever makes 1,600 red light bulbs each day. The quality control manager wants to estimate how many are defective. She randomly sampled 200 of them. Of these, 2 were found to be defective. How many light bulbs will probably have to be rejected as defective each day?

_____

Put Your Skills to the Test

1. A computer program plays a tune at random whenever it is started. There are seven different tunes in all, including "Happy Birthday" and "The Star-Spangled Banner." What is the probability that you will *not* hear "Happy Birthday" or "The Star-Spangled Banner" when you start this program?

   A. 29%

   B. 57%

   C. 71%

   D. 100%

2. A six-sided cube has two red faces, two blue, and two green. If two of these cubes are tossed two times, what is the probability of getting two red faces up on both tosses?

   A. $\frac{1}{3}$

   B. $\frac{1}{9}$

   C. $\frac{1}{18}$

   D. $\frac{1}{81}$

3. Mary Ellen has a 5-digit password on her computer. Each digit can be 1, 2, 3, 4, or 5. If Mary Ellen forgets her password, how many possible 5-digit combinations will she have to try when looking for the right one?

   A.   5

   B.   25

   C.   125

   D. 3,125

4. Three blue towels and six green towels are in Mike's clothes drier. If he pulls out one towel without looking, what is the probability that it will be blue?

   A. $\frac{1}{6}$

   B. $\frac{1}{4}$

   C. $\frac{1}{3}$

   D. $\frac{2}{3}$

5. A coin is tossed one time, and a four-color spinner, shown below, is spun once. What is the probablity that the coin will show tails and the spinner will *not* point to green?

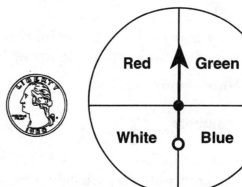

   A. $\frac{1}{2}$

   B. $\frac{1}{4}$

   C. $\frac{1}{8}$

   D. $\frac{3}{8}$

6. If a player spins the arrow 200 times, about how many times will the arrow stop on $500?

   Show your work.

   Answer: _____

7. Jake writes his name and his brother's name in the different sections of a spinning wheel.

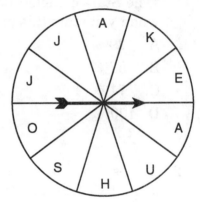

   Part A

   If he spins the arrow once, what is the probability of it landing on an A? Express your answer as a fraction, and a percent.

   Show your work.

   Fraction: _____   Percent: _____

   Part B

   How many different combinations of a consonant and a vowel would be possible if Jake spins the arrow twice?

   Show your work.

   Answer: _____

8. Create your own probability game.

unit 6

Patterns/Functions

Lesson 21: Solving Equations and Inequalities

This lesson reviews basic concepts of linear and quadratic equations and inequalities.

Expressions, Equations, and Variables

Expression: A symbol and/or number, or set of symbols and/or numbers, representing a mathematical value. The symbols and/or numbers may be connected by signs of operations. For example:

$$5x + 9 \qquad x^2 - 7 \qquad 6(3) + 8$$

Equation: A mathematical sentence that shows that two expressions are equal. For example:

$$3n + 4 = 10 \qquad 2x^3 \div 3 = 18 \qquad 14 - 6 = 8$$

Some expressions and equations have variables.

Variables: Place holders for numbers whose values are unknown. Variables are usually represented by letters.

For example, all the bold letters below are variables.

$$5\boldsymbol{x} + 9 \qquad 7 - \boldsymbol{n} \qquad C = \pi r^2 \qquad \frac{\boldsymbol{n}}{6} = 9 \qquad 3\boldsymbol{n} + 4 = 10$$

Specific letters are often (but not always) used to represent specific missing values. (You may recognize some of them.)

x or n = the value of a missing number

A = area

C = circumference

r = radius

l = length

w = width

Solving Equations with Variables

To solve equations with variable(s), you need to isolate the variable(s). To isolate the variables, you use **inverse operations**. For a review of inverse operations, see Lesson 6.

 **Example**

▶ $3n + 4 = 10$

Step 1: **Isolate the variable and find its value.**

$$3n = 10 - 4$$
$$3n = 6$$
$$n = \frac{6}{3} = 2$$

Step 2: **Check your answer by replacing the value of the variable in the equation.**

$$3n + 4 = 10$$
$$3(\mathbf{2}) + 4 = 10$$
$$6 + 4 = 10$$
$$10 = 10$$

 **PRACTICE**

Directions: Solve each equation. Check your answer.

1. $23 + y = 34$

2. $p - \frac{3}{4} = \frac{3}{4}$

3. $n - 19 = 46$

_____   _____   _____

4. Leticia has a dog-walking service. She charges each customer $2.00 per day for walking one dog, $3.00 per day for two dogs, or $4.00 per day for three dogs. Last Saturday, she earned $20.00. Five of Leticia's customers had only one dog. Two customers had two dogs.

   Write an expression that could be used to figure out how many customers (c) had three dogs. _____

Inequalities

The examples below are all inequalities.

$$x \geq 3 \qquad y < x^2 \qquad 5w \neq 100$$

Inequalities show that two expressions are not equal to each other. The relationship between inequalities is shown by one of the following symbols:

$<$ less than

$\leq$ less than or equal to

$>$ greater than

$\geq$ greater than or equal to

$\neq$ not equal to

Graphing Linear Inequalities

Linear inequalities can be graphed on a number line.

≡ Example

▶ x is less than 9 can be expressed as $x < 9$ or $9 > x$

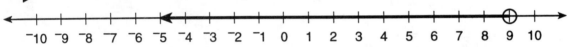

The $\bigcirc$ at 9 shows that x cannot be 9 because 9 *is not* part of the solution of the inequality.

The number line below shows that n is greater than ⁻2 and less than or equal to 5.

≡ Example

▶ $^{-}2 < n \leq 5$

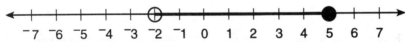

The ● at 5 shows that n can be 5 because 5 *is* part of the solution of the inequality.

What does the $\bigcirc$ at ⁻2 mean?

≣ PRACTICE

Directions: Write an inequality for each expression. Then graph each inequality.

1. R is greater than or equal to $^-1.5$ _____

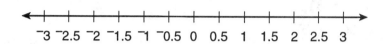

2. g is less than 20 _____

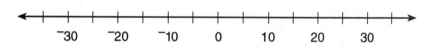

Directions: Write the expression for the inequality described by each graph. Use x for the variable.

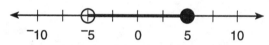

3. _____

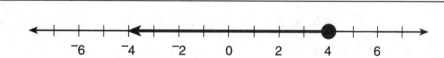

4. _____

Quadratic Equations

A **quadratic equation** is a **nonlinear equation**. A **linear equation** is an equation in which the exponent of the variable is 1 (for example, $x + 3 = 5$).

The following are examples of quadratic equations.

$$x^2 = 16 \qquad b^2 - 9 = 0 \qquad a^2 + 6a = 0 \qquad x^2 + 6x + 9 = 0$$

Quadratic equations of the form $x^2 = n$ where $n \geq 0$ can be solved by taking the square root of each side of the equation.

 Example

► $x^2 = 81$

Step 1: Since the unknown is isolated, **take the square root of each side of the equation.**

$$x^2 = 81$$
$$\sqrt{x^2} = \sqrt{81}$$
$$x = 9$$

Step 2: **Check by replacing the unknown with its value in the equation.**

$$x^2 = 81$$
$$9^2 = 81$$
$$81 = 81$$

Example

► $x^2 - 9 = 7$

Step 1: **Isolate the unknown by using inverse operations** (add the same quantity to both sides of the equation).

$$x^2 - 9 = 7$$
$$x^2 - 9 + 9 = 7 + 9$$
$$x^2 - 0 = 16$$
$$x^2 = 16$$

Step 2: **Take the square root of each side of the equation.**

$$\sqrt{x^2} = \sqrt{16}$$
$$x = 4$$

Step 3: **Check by replacing the unknown with its value in the equation.**

$$x^2 - 9 = 7$$
$$4^2 - 9 = 7$$
$$16 - 9 = 7$$
$$7 = 7$$

PRACTICE

Directions: Identify the equations in problems 1–3 as linear or quadratic.

1. $a^2 + 3a = 9$ _____

2. $x - 9 = 15$ _____

3. $9 + 6y + y^2 = 0$ _____

Directions: Solve and check your solution.

4. $x^2 + 6 = 7$ _____

5. $41 = b^2 - 8$ _____

$$+8 \qquad +8$$
$$b^2 = 49$$
$$b = 7, \; b = {}^-7$$

Lesson 22: Number and Geometric Patterns

Patterns are at the heart of much that we do in math. In a **pattern**, something is repeated. Some types of patterns you will encounter in math are number patterns, geometric patterns, and patterns that appear in graphs and tables. This lesson will review number and geometric patterns.

Number Patterns

Look at the number pattern below.

> 1, 3, 5, 7, 9, 11

This was probably one of the first odd-number patterns you encountered in math. Below is the rule that describes this pattern.

☰ Example

▶ Begin with the number one, then add two to it and to each subsequent number.

Here is another way to express the rule:

The following pattern is a little less obvious:

> 3, 12, 48, 192, 768, 3,072

Did you discover the rule that governs the pattern?

> Begin with the number 3, then multiply it and all subsequent numbers by 4.

Here is another way to express the rule:

3	12	48	192	768	3,072
3 x 4	12 x 4	48 x 4	192 x 4	768 x 4	

☰ PRACTICE

Directions: Complete the following problems.

1. What is the rule for this pattern? Write it on the lines below.

$$1, 2, 4, 7, 11, 16$$

_____

_____

_____

2. Now extend the pattern three more numbers using the rule you wrote.

1, 2, 4, 7, 11, 16, _____ , _____ , _____

3. Write your own number pattern. Write a sentence describing the rule of your pattern.

Rule: _____

_____

_____

_____

Geometric Patterns

Geometric shapes can be arranged into patterns.

 **Example**

What is the correct figure for the 13th figure in the pattern? To find the answer, you could just "count" to 13:

◻	○	◻	○
10th	11th	12th	13th

What if you needed to know the 50th piece of the pattern? You could "count" as we did above, but is there a faster and easier way?

Notice that odd-numbered figures are always ○.

Even-numbered figures are always ◻.

So the 50th figure is ◻.

Once you understand the rule, you can predict the shape of a figure anywhere in the pattern.

≣ PRACTICE

Directions: Complete the following problems.

1. Draw the appropriate figures for this pattern. (Hint: Which figure will always be a multiple of 3?)

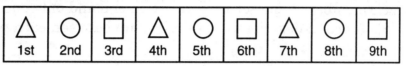

21st _____   52nd _____   99th _____

65th _____   38th _____   186th _____

2. Draw your own geometric pattern.

Write the rule that describes your pattern.

_____

_____

_____

Lesson 23: Functions and Growth Patterns

This lesson will review patterns that appear in graphs and tables.

Functions

A **function** is a rule that matches up members of one set with members of another set. Each member of one set is paired with one and only one member of the other set. The function describes the relationship between each pair.

 Example

▶ This summer, Miguel will run a refreshment stand at the beach to earn money for college. He will earn $6.75 an hour. How much money can he make in a day? A week? A month?

Number of hours worked	Money earned
1	$6.75
2	$13.50
3	$20.25
4	$27.00
•••	•••
10	$67.50
•••	•••
40	$270.00
•••	•••
160	$1080.00

The amount of money Miguel earns is a function of the number of hours he works. In other words, the amount of money he earns is *dependent upon* the number of hours he works. The relationship between hours worked and money earned is shown in the table.

The table shows two number patterns that are related in some way.

Describe each number pattern:

Number of hours worked _____

Money earned _____

This is the rule that describes the relationship between the two number patterns.

$E = \$6.75h$ (h = number of hours worked and E = total earnings)

Now use words to express the rule that describes the relationship between the two number patterns.

_____

_____

This relationship can also be expressed in a graph. The *x*-axis shows the number of hours worked and the *y*-axis shows the money earned in dollars.

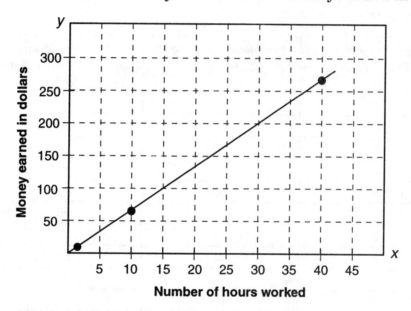

The graph of this function, or relationship, is a straight line. It is a **linear function**.

Growth Patterns

Consider the following problems:

How does the perimeter of a square change as you change the length of a side?

How does the area of a square change as you change the length of a side?

How does the area of a square change as you change the perimeter?

In order to explore these questions, let's look first at the table below. Finish the table by filling in the empty cells.

Length (in inches) of side of a square s	Perimeter (in inches) of the square $s \times 4$	Area (in square inches) of the square s^2
1	4	1
2		4
3	12	
4	16	16
5	20	25
6		36
7	28	
8	32	64
9		81
10	40	

Compare the growth of the numbers in the first column to the growth of the numbers in the second column as you look down the table.

As the numbers in the "length of side" column grow larger, the corresponding numbers in the perimeter column also grow at the same rate: The side-length value is always one-fourth as large as the perimeter value.

Now compare the first and third columns. Do the numbers in each column grow at the same rate or at a different rate? Describe the pattern.

_____

_____

_____

Next, compare the numbers in the second and third columns. Do they grow at the same rate or a different rate?

_____

_____

Can you predict how the graphs of these various number relationships will look? The graph of perimeter as a function of side length has been done for you. Plot the points for the other two graphs and then connect the points.

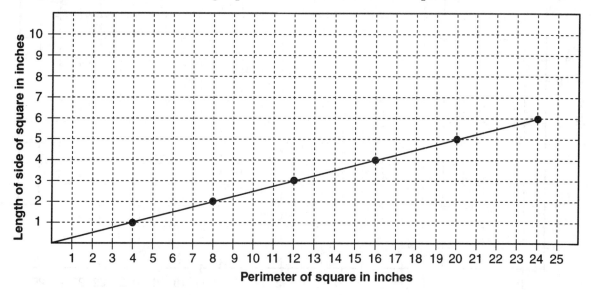

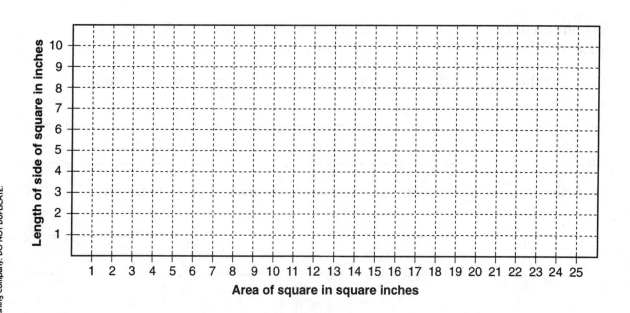

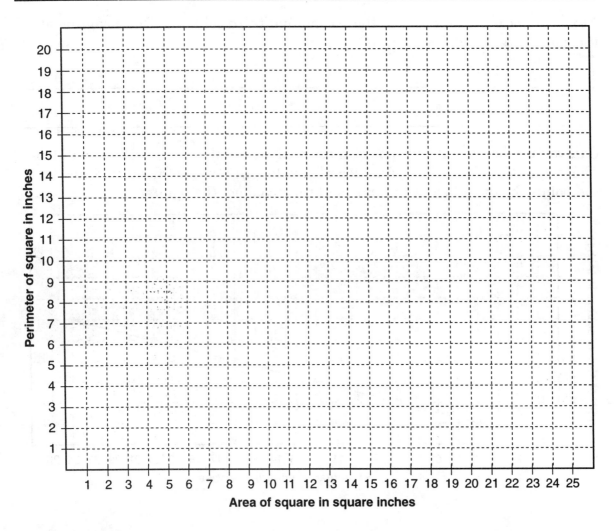

Area of square in square inches

The graph of the perimeter of a square as a function of its side length is a straight line; therefore, it is a linear function.

Describe the graph of the area of a square as a function of its side length.

_____

_____

Describe the graph of the area of a square as a function of its perimeter.

_____

_____

☰ PRACTICE

Directions: Use the graphs and/or tables on the previous pages to answer the following questions.

(P = perimeter; s = length of a side; A = area)

1. What is the general rule that describes the relationship between the length of a side (s) of a square and the square's perimeter (P)?

    _____

2. What is the general rule that describes the relationship between the length of a side (s) of a square and the square's area (A)?

    _____

3. What is the general rule that describes the relationship between the perimeter (P) of a square and the square's area (A)?

    _____

☰ Put Your Skills to the Test

1. Look at the pattern below.

   Which row would come next in the pattern?

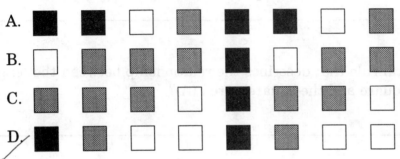

2. In the following equation, which value for *x* will make the statement true?

$$2(x + 3) - 4 = 10$$

   A. 0
   B. 1
   C. 3
   D. 4

3. Susan leases summer pasture for the horses in her riding stable. As the number of horses in the stable increases, so does her need for pasture. Use her chart to predict the amount of pasture she will need when her riding stable has reached a capacity of 15 horses.

Number of horses	Acres of land leased
3	9
6	18
12	36
15	?

   A. 45
   B. 51
   C. 72
   D. 75

172

4. Which of the following word statements could be represented by the equation $7x + 4 = 25$?

   A. 7 players scored x points in the game; one player had 4; the team scored 25 altogether.

   B. The store is open 25 hours every week; the 4 employees each work $7x$ hours every week.

   C. There are x hours in a day, $7x$ hours in a week, and 4 weeks in every month, but no month has only 25 days.

   D. 7 oranges weighing x ounces and 4 apples weighing x ounces are put into a bag weighing a total of 25 pounds.

5. Which inequality is represented by the number line below?

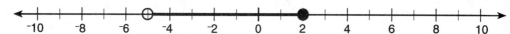

   A. $^-5 \geq n \geq 2$
   B. $2 > {}^-5 > n$
   C. $^-5 < n \geq 2$
   D. $^-5 < n \leq 2$

6. Graph the following inequality on the number line below.

$$x \geq {}^-3$$

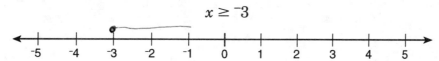

7. The box shown casts a shadow that is 3 feet long. What is the vertical length of the box?

   Show your work or explain in words.

   Answer:_____

   $5^2 \times 3^2 + x^2 =$

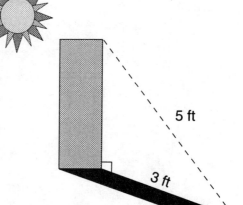

5 ft

3 ft

8. Jenny sold 150 hot dogs and 225 bags of peanuts at the baseball game on Saturday. She made a total of $600. Jenny sold each hot dog for $2.50.

Part A

Write an equation you can use to find the cost, c, of each bag of peanuts.

Equation: _$1.00_____

Part B

Solve your equation to find the cost of one bag of peanuts.

Show your work.

Answer: _____

appendix

General Tips for Taking Math Tests
New York Learning Standards for Mathematics

General Tips for Taking Math Tests

The only guaranteed way to pass any math test is to learn the math. If you learn everything in this book, you should ace the state test. Here are a few general tips to keep in mind on test day.

TIP 1: Take your time.

The strategies that follow will require that you spend some extra time as you're taking the test. This will be time well spent. If you practice these strategies in advance, and apply the strategies when you take the test, you'll have a much better chance of passing.

TIP 2: Make two passes through the test.

If everybody in your class went through the test and circled the ten hardest problems, each person would pick a different set. What this means is that, for you personally, the hard problems will be mixed in with the easy problems. You need to pay attention to this difficulty issue. Our advice is to make two passes through the test.

On the first pass, skip every problem that seems hard to you. Go all the way from the first question to the last question working *only* the easy problems. You might skip ten questions or you might skip thirty questions. The important thing is to solve *all* of the easy problems before you get frustrated by the hard problems. As you do this, stop and check your work on every problem. Don't think you have the correct answer just because it's one of the choices. *Stop* and *check your work*. Then continue to the next question.

On the second pass, solve the harder problems. Remember, you have plenty of time— use it. Try one way and then another to solve each problem.

TIP 3: DO NOT leave any blanks on your answer sheet.

No matter how tired you are at the end of the test, go back and check to make sure you answered every question.If you do not know the answer, then narrow down your choices as much as possible and guess.

TIP 4: Remember to take a step-by-step approach to story and application problems.

In the workbook, you learned how to solve word problems by taking things one step at a time. Here's a quick review of those steps.

Make sure you understand the question. Try to see the operation that is taking place, so that you can pull the math from the problem. Reread the problem to make sure your math works. Do the math. Then, as always, check your work.

TIP 5: Learn to work backwards.

What if you can't figure out what to do? There may be a few problems where you try and try but can't find the solution. With practice, you can spot a few problems where it's possible to "plug in" the answer choices and work the problems backwards.

Example

To earn a grade of B in science, Nancy needs to score an average of 80 on three tests. On the first test, she scored 85. On the second test, she scored 70. To earn a B, what score does Nancy need on the third test?

A. 70

B. 75

C. 80

D. 85

First, underline the question part of the problem, "what score does Nancy need on the third test?" To work backwards, take one of the choices and try it. If B is the correct answer, Nancy's scores would be 85, 70, and 75. What is the average of these three scores?

_____

Since choice B is not big enough, you can cross it out. You can also cross out choice A, because that's even smaller. The correct answer has to be either C or D. If C is the answer, Nancy's scores would be 85, 70, and 80. What is the average of these three scores?

_____

If you plug in D, Nancy's scores would be 85, 70, and 85. What is the average of these three scores?

_____

TIP 6: Cross out careless choices before you guess.

Sometimes you can't even plug in the choices. Before you guess, check the answers carefully and cross out careless choices.

Example

Martha bought a radio on sale at a 15% discount. If the retail price is normally $60.00, how much did Martha pay for the radio?

A. $ 4.00

B. $ 9.00

C. $45.00

D. $51.00

Look at choice A. If a radio is normally $60.00, do you think Martha is going to get it for only $4.00? Of course not. Cross out A. How about B? Not. Cross it out. Now guess between C and D. If you do this on ten problems, you'll guess about five of them correct.

TIP 7: On test day, relax.

If you've practiced the material in *Sharpen Up on New York Mathematics*, *Book 8*, your math skills will be "built-in" by test day. You won't be worried because you'll know that you're prepared. You can relax knowing that you're ready to do your best.

New York Learning Standards for Mathematics, Grade 8

Sharpen Up on New York Mathematics, Book 8, addresses the seven key ideas of the *New York Learning Standards for Mathematics* listed on pages 178–180.

Key Ideas and Performance Indicators	*Sharpen Up Lesson(s)*
Mathematical Reasoning	
1. Students use mathematical reasoning to analyze mathematical situations, make conjectures, gather evidence, and construct an argument.	
Students:	
• apply a variety of reasoning strategies.	
• make and evaluate conjectures and arguments using appropriate language.	1–23
• make conclusions based on inductive reasoning.	
• justify conclusions involving simple and compound (i.e., and/or) statements.	
Number and Numeration	
2. Students use number sense and numeration to develop an understanding of the multiple uses of numbers in the real world, the use of numbers to communicate mathematically, and the use of numbers in the development of mathematical ideas.	
Students:	
• understand, represent, and use numbers in a variety of equivalent forms (integer, fraction, decimal, percent, exponential, expanded and scientific notation).	1
• understand and apply ratios, proportions, and percents through a wide variety of hands-on explorations.	8
• develop an understanding of number theory (primes, factors, and multiples).	2
• recognize order relations for decimals, integers, and rational numbers.	3
Operations	
3. Students use mathematical operations and relationships among them to understand mathematics.	
Students:	
• add, subtract, multiply, and divide fractions, decimals, and integers.	4
• explore and use the operations dealing with roots and powers.	5
• use grouping symbols (parentheses) to clarify the intended order of operations.	6
• apply the associative, commutative, distributive, inverse, and identity properties.	7
• demonstrate an understanding of operational algorithms (procedures for adding, subtracting, etc.).	6
• develop appropriate proficiency with facts and algorithms.	6
• apply concepts of ratio and proportion to solve problems.	8

continued on next page

Key Ideas and Performance Indicators	Sharpen Up Lesson(s)
Modeling/Multiple Representation	
4. Students use mathematical modeling/multiple representation to provide a means of presenting, interpreting, communicating, and connecting mathematical information and relationships.	
Students:	
• visualize, represent, and transform two- and three-dimensional shapes.	10
• use maps and scale drawings to represent real objects or places.	14
• use the coordinate plane to explore geometric ideas.	13
• represent numerical relationships in one- and two-dimensional graphs.	13, 21
• use variables to represent relationships.	21
• use concrete materials and diagrams to describe the operation of real world processes and systems.	19
• develop and explore models that do and do not rely on chance	20, 21
• investigate both two- and three-dimensional transformations.	15
• use appropriate tools to construct and verify geometric relationships.	9
• develop procedures for basic geometric constructions.	9
Measurement	
5. Students use measurement in both metric and English measure to provide a major link between the abstractions of mathematics and the real world in order to describe and compare objects and data.	
Students:	
• estimate, make, and use measurements in real-world situations.	17
• select appropriate standard and nonstandard measurement units and tools to measure a desired degree of accuracy.	17
• develop measurement skills and informally derive and apply formulas in direct measurement activities.	18
• use statistical methods and measures of central tendencies to display, describe, and compare data.	19
• explore and produce graphic representations of data using calculators/computers.	19
• develop critical judgment for the reasonableness of measurement.	17

continued on next page

Key Ideas and Performance Indicators	*Sharpen Up* Lesson(s)
Uncertainty	
6. Students use ideas of uncertainty to illustrate that mathematics involve more than exactness when dealing with everyday situations.	
Students:	
• use estimation to check the reasonableness of results obtained by computation, algorithms, or the use of technology.	6, 15, 18
• use estimation to solve problems for which exact answers are inappropriate.	6, 15, 18
• estimate the probability of events.	20
• use simulation techniques to estimate probabilities.	20
• determine probabilities of independent and mutually exclusive events.	20
Patterns/Functions	
7. Students use patterns and functions to develop mathematical power, appreciate the true beauty of mathematics, and construct generalizations that describe patterns simply and efficiently.	
Students:	
• recognize, describe, and generalize a wide variety of patterns and functions.	22
• describe and represent patterns and functional relationships using tables, charts and graphs, algebraic expressions, rules, and verbal descriptions.	23
• develop methods to solve basic linear and quadratic equations.	21
• develop an understanding of functions and functional relationships: that change in one quantity (variable) results in change in another.	23
• verify results of substituting variables.	21
• apply the concepts of similarity in relevant situations.	12
• use properties of polygons to classify them.	10
• explore relationships involving points, lines, angles, and planes.	9
• develop and apply the Pythagorean principle in the solution of problems.	11
• explore and develop basic concepts of right triangle trigonometry.	16
• use patterns and functions to represent and solve problems.	22, 23